The recent attempt to remove Justice William O. Douglas from the Supreme Court has prompted the noted constitutional authority Irving Brant to write the first comprehensive study of the impeachment clause of the U.S. Constitution. Beginning with the trial of Senator William Blount of Tennessee in 1797 (for plotting with England to invade Spanish Florida), Mr. Brant examines the doctrine of impeachment through its twelve cases in American history. Nearly all of these articles of impeachment, he believes, were improperly drawn up by the House of Representatives, which has distorted impeachment by honest error, maladministration, political motivation, or arbitrary behavior. He charges Congress with attempting to pattern impeachment on what it was in England under the Stuart rulers: twisting the "high crimes and misdemeanors" phrase of the constitutional article into an unrestricted power to impeach for any cause. The author concludes with a prescription for a remedy to the misuse of impeachment that was foreshadowed by the lawyers who defended Andrew Johnson.

Dollars and Sense (1933)

Storm over the Constitution (1936)

James Madison: The Virginia Revolutionist (1941)

The Nationalist (1948)

Father of the Constitution (1950)

Secretary of State (1953)

The President (1956)

Commander in Chief (1961)

Road to Peace and Freedom (1943)

The New Poland (1946)

Friendly Cove (1963)

The Bill of Rights (1965)

James Madison and American Nationalism (1967)

The Fourth President: A Life of James Madison (1969)

IMPEACHMENT

Trials and Errors

IMPEACHMENT

Trials and Errors

IRVING BRANT

ALFRED·A·KNOPF

New York / 1972

Library of Congress Cataloging in Publication Data

Brant, Irving, 1885–   Impeachment: trials and errors.
Includes bibliographical references.
1. Impeachments—U.S.   I. Title.
KF8781.B7   347′.73′14   71–171134
ISBN 0–394–47326–4

Manufactured in the United States of America

First Edition

Contents

IMPEACHMENT

Trials and Errors

CHAPTER I

THE CONSTITUTION
ON IMPEACHMENT

To the average American with a fair knowledge of history, the word "impeachment" has until recently brought to mind only the unsuccessful attempt to remove Andrew Johnson from the Presidency shortly after the Civil War. The impeachers lacked one vote of the necessary two-thirds majority in the Senate. Their near-success, plus the fact that Johnson was a self-educated merchant-tailor, has led to general disparagement of him as President. This low estimate has been tempered only by the verdict of school historians that, in clumsy fashion, Johnson was trying to pursue the Lincoln policy of postwar reconciliation between North and South.

For more than half a century of postcollege study that was largely devoted to constitutional history, the author of this book held the popular view of the Johnson impeachment: that although it was well for the country that the attempt failed, it reflected Johnson's incompetence as President. This deeply embedded concept vanished in a flash in

(3)

1970, when the author read the official record of the trial in the 1868 *Congressional Globe*.

The record shows that regardless of the merits or demerits of Andrew Johnson, the attempt to remove him from office by impeachment was the most insidious assault on constitutional government in the nation's history. It was carried on in direct violation of the limitations deliberately placed in the Constitution to prevent such a happening. If it had been successful and had been accepted as a precedent, it would have converted a government of divided powers, of checks and balances, into a congressional dictatorship.

Thomas Jefferson called a legislative tyranny the worst of all tyrannies. James Madison, in presenting his Bill of Rights to Congress in 1789, said that the guarantees of liberty must be leveled chiefly "against the Legislative [branch of government] for it is the most powerful, and most likely to be abused, because it is under the least control." All such warnings were disregarded by the men of passion who ruled Congress after the Civil War, and only by the margin of a single vote did they fail to reduce the constitutional edifice to rubble.

The first impeachment after that of President Johnson took place in 1876, when Secretary of War W. W. Belknap was put on trial for corruption in office. Manifestly guilty, he escaped conviction on a technicality that lay well within the bounds of legitimate differences of opinion. With no sectional passions involved, the limitations of the Constitution were observed.

Since then, in cases separated by long intervals, the excesses of Andrew Johnson's trial have been revived and gradually extended. This extension process began, not under the stress of nationwide emotional upheavals, but in a virtually automatic stretching of congressional power with no evil intent. It culminated in a new and even more dangerous blend of hot passion and cold purpose, in the attempt to remove Associate Justice William O. Douglas from the United States Supreme Court.

The motives for this attempt are obvious. Hatred was engendered by Douglas's thirty-one-year championship of civil rights and liberties, both on the Court and in numerous books, articles, and lectures. He also became the focus of resentment precipitated by the Senate's rejection of President Nixon's nominees to the Supreme Court, Clement Haynsworth and G. Harrold Carswell. Finally and most fundamental was the purpose of driving Douglas off the bench to help Nixon reshape the Court to fit his own philosophy of the law.

The full extent of the change in attitudes toward congressional powers of impeachment is evident when one compares the words of the Constitution with those of Republican Minority Leader Gerald C. Ford in his speech of April 15, 1970, setting the impeachment proceedings against Douglas in motion. The constitutional scope of the power to impeach is found in Article II, section 4:

> *The President, Vice President and all civil officers of the United States, shall be removed from Office on Impeachment for, and Conviction of, Treason, Bribery, or other high Crimes and Misdemeanors.*

Ford, however, presented this description of constitutional power:

"What, then, is an impeachable offense?

"The only honest answer is that an impeachable offense is whatever a majority of the House of Representatives considers it to be at a given moment in history; conviction results from whatever offense or offenses two-thirds of the other body considers to be sufficiently serious to require removal of the accused from office."

Put more plainly, Ford said that under the Constitution, the President, Vice President, and any civil officer of the United States can be removed from office at the pleasure of a majority of the House of Representatives and two thirds of the Senate. It is impossible to imagine a wider gap between the Constitution's and Representative Ford's description of the impeachment power.

Chiefly to clear the air, the House of Representatives passed an impeachment resolution in 1970 which contained no specific charges against Justice Douglas. The House Committee on the Judiciary, in a special subcommittee headed by Emanuel Celler, investigated the charges made by those seeking impeachment. In a 924-page report the subcommittee cleared Justice Douglas completely, finding no factual basis for removal even under Congressman Ford's catchall conception of congressional power. The report went further and specifically rejected Ford's conception. For the first time in a hundred years, it turned the power of impeachment back toward the limitations intended by the framers of the Constitution. If the restricted concept is adhered to, it will be a more important result than the retention of any particular man on the Supreme Court. This return to the sense of the Constitution emphasizes the need for a thorough reexploration of the history of impeachment, and especially of the Founding Fathers' deviations from British precedent in framing the Constitution.

First we should bring together all the constitutional provisions dealing with or having a possible bearing on the impeachment process. They are scattered through the document in no particular order and will be presented here as they occur. First is the assignment of power to the two houses. Article I, section 2:

> *The House of Representatives shall . . . have the sole power of Impeachment.*

Article I, section 3:

> *The Senate shall have the sole power to try all impeachments.*

These clauses point to a common error in speech. People often speak of "being impeached" as being removed from office by impeachment. Instead, "impeachment" is a formal accusation by the House of Representatives, akin to a grand jury indictment. Article I, section 3 also fixes senatorial procedures in impeachment:

> *When sitting for that purpose, they shall be on oath or affirmation. When the President of the United States is tried, the Chief Justice shall preside: And no person shall be convicted without the concurrence of two-thirds of the members present.*

Historically in England, persons impeached by the House of Commons and convicted by the House of Lords were subject to removal from office, fines, imprisonment, or death. In theory they still are, but British impeachments have long since disappeared. In our Constitution, punishment is sharply limited. To continue with section 3:

> *Judgment in cases of Impeachment shall not extend further than to removal from office, and disqualification to hold and enjoy any office of honor, trust or profit under the*

United States, but the party convicted shall nevertheless be liable and subject to indictment, trial, judgment, and punishment according to law.

Another provision deprives the President of any power to intervene in the proceedings, which are most likely to be directed against his appointees to office. Article II, section 2:

The President . . . shall have power to grant reprieves and pardons for offences against the United States, except in cases of Impeachment.

Then comes the all-important clause quoted earlier: Article II, section 4, which determines who can be impeached (the President, Vice President, and all civil officers of the United States) and for what offenses (treason, bribery, or other high crimes and misdemeanors).

An incidental provision on another subject gains importance because even more emphatically than other clauses, it classifies impeachment as a criminal proceeding, thereby putting it within the guarantees of due process of law and reducing to nonsense the frequent claim that impeachment is simply a civil inquest into general fitness for office. Article III, section 2:

The trial of all crimes, except in cases of Impeachment, shall be by jury.

The Constitution contains no other reference to impeachment, nor does it provide any other method of removing public officials who possess tenure during good behavior. Running through all the clauses on impeachment are words and phrases connoting criminality. Nowhere is there a reference to removal for misbehavior of a noncriminal nature. The opening paragraph of the judiciary article, however, contains one sentence which has been construed by some (most recently by Minority Leader Ford) to extend the impeachment power over judges to any conduct that the House and Senate may regard as misbehavior. Article III, section 1, opens as follows:

> *The judicial power of the United States shall be vested in one Supreme Court, and in such inferior courts as the Congress may from time to time ordain and establish. The judges, both of the supreme and inferior courts, shall hold their offices during good behavior.*

On the principle that a positive assertion implies a correlative negative, this has been taken by some lawyers and lawmakers to mean that a judge may be removed from office for anything which two thirds of the Senate may construe to be "ill behavior." If so, the Constitution might as well contain the simple wording: "Judges shall hold office at the pleasure of the Senate." That principle was expressly discussed and rejected in the debate which brought the "high crimes and misdemeanors" clause into the Constitution. However, let us examine the "removal for ill behavior" doctrine in the most favorable possible light—that is, in the words of its advocates. The first discussion of it occurred in the trial of Justice Samuel Chase in 1805, which was a political prosecution by the Jefferson administration, based on Chase's arbitrary, biased enforcement of the Sedition Act of 1798 in his circuit court duties. The last discussion was in the 1970 attempt to impeach Justice Douglas.

From the very first, impeachment trials have been prosecuted by "Managers" (usually five) appointed by the House of Representatives from its own members. In the action against Justice Douglas, Minority Leader Ford and his lawyer, Bethel B. Kelley of Detroit, took the place of official

Managers. Ford made his charges on the floor of the House; Kelley supported them in written briefs submitted to the investigating committee. Both laid heavy emphasis upon the "good behavior" clause, making it indeed the crux of their position.

Kelley, quoting what was said on that subject back in the trial of Justice Chase, introduced the passage with the words "Said the managers: . . ." He thereby created the impression that the Managers, working in unison, made the absence of "good behavior" the principal ground of action. But actually the argument was advanced by Manager Joseph H. Nicholson almost at the end of the trial, in a last attempt to salvage a losing case. This, of course, does not affect the validity or invalidity of Kelley's argument. However, it does destroy his implication that the primary emphasis in the Chase trial was on the "good behavior" clause, and that the clause consequently has a heightened claim to acceptance as an alternative to removal for "treason, bribery, or other high crimes and misdemeanors"—the only grounds specified in the Constitution.

What is the origin of the term "high crimes and misdemeanors"? It was first used, according to historian Henry Hallam, by Edward III of England in 1376, when he ordered Parliament to impeach Lord Latimer. Commons and Lords obeyed as a matter of course, and the term continued to be used in impeachment proceedings during the long, slow, and generally stormy rise of Parliament from subservience to supremacy over kings.

Because of the doctrine that the king can do no wrong, the actual battles were fought between Parliament and the king's ministers. The king ruled the courts and judges did his bidding. Impeachment—after Parliament gained sufficient strength to employ it independently—was an instrument by which the legislative branch could rid the government of lawbreaking ministers or of judges who sheltered them at the king's behest. The system paralleled the common law, and carried the death penalty whenever the House of Lords chose to inflict it.

Hallam records in his *Constitutional History of England* that impeachment fell into disuse after the conviction of the Duke of Suffolk in 1449. This was due in part to the loss of the control Parliament had had over Lancastrian kings, in part to "the preference the Tudor princes had given to bills of attainder or of pains and penalties, when they wished to turn the arm of parliament against an obnoxious subject."

Impeachment was revived in 1620, according to Hallam, when the House of Commons proceeded against Sir Giles Montpesson for misusing a patent. (He substituted base metals for gold or silver and was "forever held an infamous person.") Forgetting the details of ancient process, the House of Commons undertook both to impeach and to try the accused. The Lords checked this and took over the trial and punishment. The Commons at the time, says Hallam, were justly aroused to wrath "against that shameless corruption which characterizes the reign of James [I] beyond every other in our history." He continues:

"But in the midst of these laudable proceedings they were hurried by the passions of the moment to an act of most unwarrantable violence. It came to the knowledge of the house that one Floyd, a gentleman confined in the Fleet prison, had used some slighting words about the elector palatine and his wife. It appeared, in aggravation, that he was a Roman Catholic. Nothing could exceed the fury into which the commons were thrown by this very insignificant story . . . [and they] fixed upon the most degrading punishment they could devise."

Forced by protests from both the king and the House of

Lords, the Commons retracted their final action and turned Floyd over to the Lords, who proceeded to outdo the Commons in ferocity. They ordered Floyd pilloried, branded, whipped at a cart's tail across town (the king remitted this), and imprisoned for life. Hallam comments: "The cold-blooded deliberate policy of the lords is still more disgusting than the wild fury of the lower house."

Such were the practices that the framers of our Constitution must have intended to endorse and perpetuate, if the House Managers of American impeachments are correct about the sanctity of British precedents. The framers knew the history of impeachment, both in its valid principles and in the manifold violations of them by overzealous Commons and Lords. They knew impeachment was a criminal proceeding to punish crimes and misdemeanors and relieve society of the effects of criminal conduct by officers of government. They held to the same procedures described in the Vinerian Lectures of Professor Richard Wooddesson of Oxford, published in 1792–4. Said this noted legal authority about the purpose and nature of the law of impeachment:

"As to the trial itself, it must, of course, vary in external ceremony, but differs not in essentials from criminal prosecutions before inferior courts. The same rules of evidence, the same legal notions of crimes and punishments, prevail. For impeachments are not formed to alter the law, but to carry it into more effectual execution, where *it might be obstructed by the views of too powerful delinquents,* or not easily discerned in the ordinary course of jurisdiction, by reason of the peculiar quality of alleged crimes. The judgment therefore is to be such as is warranted by legal principles or precedents. In capital cases the mere stated sentence [death] is to be specifically pronounced."

That exposition of British practice sufficiently explains the numerous references to crime and punishment in the impeachment clauses of our Constitution. Impeachment is a special form of punishment for crime, designed to remove high-ranking offenders from the protection of the executive branch or of subservient courts. The limited punishment and strict definition of grounds of impeachment are guards against the excesses that have marked its use in England.

At the opening of the Philadelphia Convention of 1787, the Virginia Plan, written by James Madison, furnished the principles and embodied the general form of the government that took shape under the united labors of the delegates. Submitted on May 29, debated and revised during four strenuous weeks, these resolutions were referred on July 26 to a five-man Committee of Detail. Its membership included three future justices of the Supreme Court—John Rutledge of South Carolina, James Wilson of Pennsylvania, and (Chief Justice) Oliver Ellsworth of Connecticut—as well as Edmund Randolph, governor of Virginia, and Nathaniel Gorham of Massachusetts. The principal working paper of the committee was a draft constitution written by Wilson, on which committee emendations were made in the handwriting of Chairman Rutledge. On August 6, the day to which the convention recessed, the committee reported the full draft of a constitution not greatly different from the final document.

Madison's Virginia Plan had provided for a "National Judiciary . . . to consist of one or more supreme tribunals, and of inferior tribunals to be chosen by the National Legislature, to hold their offices during good behavior." On July 18 this clause "to hold their offices during good behavior" had been agreed to without opposition. Two days later the convention had entered into a long debate on the impeachability of the Executive, and in the course of discussion a distinction was attempted between a magistrate with fixed tenure and one holding office "during good behavior." Said

Rufus King of Massachusetts, arguing that the Executive should be removed only by refusal of reelection:

"It had been said that the Judiciary would be impeachable. But it should have been remembered at the same time that the Judiciary hold their places not for a limited time, but during good behavior. It is necessary, therefore, that a forum should be established for trying misbehavior."

The convention did not establish "misbehavior" as a constitutional ground of removal. It would have been so established, however, without even using the word, if the convention had approved a motion made by John Dickinson of Delaware on August 27. That day the convention took up the following section of the judiciary article reported by the Committee of Detail in its August 6 draft:

"The Judges of the Supreme Court, and of the inferior courts, shall hold their offices during good behavior."

Dickinson moved to add, "after the words 'good behavior,' the words 'provided that they may be removed by the Executive on the applications of the Senate and House of Representatives.'" Elbridge Gerry of Massachusetts seconded.

This motion was based on a British procedure called "removal by address," established by Parliament in 1701 in the Act of Settlement that governed the accession of Queen Anne to the throne. Eighty years of Stuart misrule had given way in the "Glorious Revolution" of 1688 to parliamentary and monarchic reform. However, England was still saddled with Stuart judges holding office "during the pleasure of the crown"—a hated and demoralizing system. So Parliament enacted a law providing that judges should hold their offices during good behavior, "but upon the address of both Houses of Parliament it may be lawful [for the monarch] to remove them."

It was this procedure, historically unrelated to impeachment, that Dickinson sought to graft onto the "good behavior" clause. His motion met instant protest, centering naturally on its arbitrary nature. Madison recorded the debate:

"Mr. Gouverneur Morris thought it a contradiction in terms to say that the Judges should hold their offices during good behavior and yet be removable without a trial. Besides it was fundamentally wrong to subject Judges to so arbitrary an authority."

Roger Sherman, the Connecticut shoemaker turned judge, saw no contradiction or impropriety in such a constitutional regulation of the judiciary: "He observed that a like provision was contained in the British Statutes."

The reply came from British-born James Wilson, Pennsylvania professor of law and later justice of the Supreme Court:

"Mr. Wilson considered such a provision in the British Government as less dangerous than here, the House of Lords and House of Commons being less likely to concur on the same occasion. Chief Justice Holt [the great liberal jurist of the William and Mary period], he remarked, had *successively* offended by his independent conduct, both Houses of Parliament. The judges would be in a bad situation if made to depend on every gust of faction which might prevail in the two branches of our Government."

Governor Edmund Randolph of Virginia "opposed the motion as weakening too much the independence of the judges."

The vote, with three states unrecorded for lack of a quorum: Aye—Connecticut. No—New Hampshire, Pennsylvania, Delaware, Maryland, Virginia, South Carolina, Georgia.

Although the protests against "removal by address" emphasized the absence of a trial, that was incidental. Passion, if unrestrained by constitutional safeguards, can always work its will. Any House of Representatives empowered to impeach, and any Senate empowered to convict, for any conduct the two Houses regard as misbehavior, would possess a virtual power *to remove by address* to the President *without making the address.* In such a Congress, if swayed by passion, trial would be a farce. Under the construction of tenure "during good behavior" made by Manager Nicholson in 1805, and by Gerald Ford, acting as Manager in 1970, House and Senate would have a power which the framers of the Constitution specifically refused to place in the combined hands of the House, Senate, and President of the United States.

Of such dangerous irrationality is the whole "during good behavior" argument built. In reality, the phrase was generally used in the Constitutional Convention, not with emphasis on the qualifications of judges, but as an accurate substitute for the term "for life," in debating whether the tenure of the President should be indefinite (as Hamilton and some others wished) or for a fixed term of years. The point here is that, seven states to one, the framers voted down the only attempt to use "during good behavior" as an instrument in itself for removal from office.

Given this fact, what is left of the contention that the impeachment clauses themselves were intended to establish a power of removal for any conduct regarded by the Senate as misbehavior? The debate and action on impeachment had two places of origin—in articles regarding the executive department and those regarding the judiciary. The August 6 draft of the Constitution contained the following clause concerning the President:

"He shall be removed from office on impeachment by the House of Representatives, and conviction in the Supreme Court, of treason, bribery, or corruption."

Thus the Supreme Court was to try the President on impeachment by the House; the draft contained no provision for impeachment of judges. On August 20 Gouverneur Morris moved that a council of state consisting of the Chief Justice and five secretaries of departments be set up to assist the President. This clause followed:

"Each of the officers abovementioned shall be liable to impeachment and removal from office for neglect of duty, malversation, or corruption."

This motion had the peculiar effect of making the Chief Justice subject to removal by his own colleagues, for whom no impeachment process had been provided. As a corrective Gerry moved that the Committee of Detail, to which the Morris motion was referred, be instructed to report the "mode of trying the Supreme Judges in cases of impeachment." Two days later the Committee of Detail recommended the following addition to the judiciary article:

"The judges of the supreme court shall be triable by the Senate, on impeachment by the House of Representatives."

At that stage the President, on impeachment, was triable by the Supreme Court. On August 27 the provision came up for impeaching the President "for treason, bribery or corruption." It was postponed on motion of Morris, who regarded the Supreme Court as "an improper tribunal" to try the Executive. All these pending motions were referred on August 31 to an eleven-man Committee on Unfinished Parts. On September 4 this group submitted an amendment shifting the trial of the President from the Supreme Court to the Senate and eliminating "or corruption" from the grounds of impeachment.

Final decisions on impeachment were made on September 8. Without controversy, the convention extended liability to include "the Vice President and other civil officers of the United States." That covered the judges. By a vote of nine states to two, impeachment trials were transferred from the Supreme Court to the Senate. The only controversy related to grounds of impeachment. The clause as it came from the committee read as follows:

"He [the President] shall be removed from his office on impeachment by the House of Representatives, and conviction by the Senate, for treason, or bribery."

George Mason of Virginia promptly asked:

"Why is this provision restrained to treason and bribery only? Treason as defined in the Constitution will not reach many great and dangerous offenses. Hastings [governor of India, lately impeached and then awaiting trial] is not guilty of Treason. Attempts to subvert the Constitution may not be treason as above defined. As bills of attainder which have saved the British Constitution are forbidden, it is necessary to extend the power of impeachments."*

Mason moved to add, after "bribery," the words "or maladministration." Elbridge Gerry seconded him.

Madison objected. "So vague a term," he said, "will be equivalent to a tenure during the pleasure of the Senate." Mason gave up his attempt. He withdrew "maladministration," Madison recorded, and substituted "other high crimes and misdemeanors against the State."

Here is conclusive proof that the term "high crimes and

---

* This was by no means an approval of bills of attainder for the United States; they had been unanimously prohibited. The words "which saved the British Constitution" needed no explication. Rushworth's *Historical Collections,* with which educated Americans were familiar, devoted its entire final volume of 786 pages to the trial and execution of the Earl of Strafford, Charles I's favorite minister, through a bill of attainder. Before attainder was resorted to, impeachment was attempted and then abandoned, partly for lack of proof that the Earl's violations of the constitution had been criminal, partly because the king was threatening to interfere with the trial. Charles had power to set aside the sentence of death, but was advised by Strafford himself not to do so lest he lose his throne—which he did lose soon afterward, along with his head.

misdemeanors" was not meant to be synonymous with "maladministration." Impeachment was to be grounded on high criminality. That was made even more evident later the same day, when the words "against the State" were changed to "against the United States"—an alteration, wrote Madison, designed "to remove ambiguity."

The original wording "against the State" could mean offenses against both state and federal law, or against state law alone. The words "against the United States" narrowed the application. They were eliminated, however, by the Committee on Style and Arrangement, whose work was performed almost entirely by Gouverneur Morris. Although the committee was not authorized to make any changes in meaning, the change clearly lengthened the reach of impeachment to major violations of either federal or state law. This may have been intentional; it may have been accidental; in either case it was commendable.

What about the word "high," prefixed to "crimes" but not to "misdemeanors"? Does it mean "high crimes and high misdemeanors," or does it mean "high crimes and any sort of misdemeanors"? If the latter, a justice of the Supreme Court can be impeached and removed from office for forfeiting bail on an automobile parking ticket. Yearning for that broad interpretation, but not quite willing to make it, Minority Leader Ford said in his "impeachment" speech of April 15, 1970:

"There are pages upon pages of learned argument whether the adjective 'high' modifies 'misdemeanors' as well as 'crimes,' and over what, indeed, constitutes a 'high misdemeanor.' "

Learned argument on the word "high" actually does appear for "pages upon pages" (two pages in all) in the mammoth records of American impeachment trials. One is an able argument by counsel for Judge Chase in 1805, designed to show that impeachable misdemeanors must be high; the other is a reply by House Manager Caesar Rodney: "We would willingly have conceded the point, and saved him his labor and his breath."

There has, however, been vigorous argument and strong division over what constitutes a "high misdemeanor." Its meaning is not defined in the Constitution, nor was it discussed in the debate on impeachment in the Federal Convention. Putting together the various grounds of impeachment that were formally placed before the convention, either by individual motion or in committee reports, we find the following: maladministration (objected to and withdrawn), neglect of duty, malversation, corruption, treason, bribery. To these might be added certain words used in debate. Madison on July 20 "thought it indispensable that some provision should be made for defending the Community against the incapacity, negligence or perfidy of the chief Magistrate." Gouverneur Morris added: "Charles II was bribed by Louis XVI. The Executive ought therefore to be impeachable for treachery; corrupting his electors, and incapacity were other causes of impeachment."

Perfidy and treachery of the sort Madison and Morris had in mind would be a form of treason. Malversation is fraud in office. Corruption implies criminal acts. Of the entire list of offenses casually mentioned in convention debate, only "incapacity" and "neglect of duty" are nonindictable as felonies or high misdemeanors. Neither of these was formally put forward. Gross and willful neglect of duty (such as perverse refusal to hold court at times prescribed by law), would be a violation of the oath of office. Selling justice would be an even grosser violation. These assuredly would be high crimes or high misdemeanors, either by statute or common law, or as violations of the oath of office. Thus the list of offenses finally given in the Constitution is in harmony with Madison's successful contention that maladministration as a specified ground of impeachment would be equivalent to "tenure during the pleasure of the Senate," both of which were condemned and rejected by the framers.

Superficially, but only superficially, a remark by Madison in the First Congress of the United States appears to contradict the position he took on maladministration in the Constitutional Convention. In debating a bill to create a department of foreign affairs, some members took the position that because consent of the Senate was required to appoint the department head, its consent was likewise required to remove him. Madison combated this contention, arguing that the appointment and removal of officers was an executive function; the participation of the Senate in the appointment was a specific exception from that principle, and Congress had no authority to make other exceptions unless they were set forth in the Constitution. To require Senate consent to the displacement of a department head, he said, would destroy the real responsibility of the President without leaving "even the shadow."

This was powerful reasoning and carried the day, but not without a hard struggle. An advocate of Senate participation in removals asked what would happen if the President removed meritorious officers. For such an abuse of power, Madison replied, "he will be impeachable by the House, before the Senate for such an act of maladministration, for I contend that wanton removal of meritorious officers would subject him to impeachment and removal from his own high trust."

This remark was joyfully quoted by the impeachers of President Andrew Johnson, who had removed Secretary of War Stanton in defiance of a law (enacted to protect Stanton) prohibiting the removal of Cabinet officers without senatorial consent. The House Managers carefully omitted Madison's next words: "But what can be his motives for displacing a worthy man? It must be that he may fill the place with an unworthy creature of his own." By ascribing "wanton removal of meritorious officers" to a deliberate purpose of appointing an "unworthy creature of his own," Madison implanted the element of criminality—violation of the oath of office—into a normal political procedure. But he took inadequate account of human nature. A political faction whose favorite is ousted is capable of looking upon any successor as an "unworthy creature." So, even though Madison stated the case in terms that implied violation of the President's oath of office, his argument made the tenure of the President, in relation to removals, depend on the "pleasure of the Senate"—the very thing that caused him and the convention to reject maladministration as a ground of impeachment. His remark, imputing criminality to a particular act of maladministration, carries not the slightest indication that he regarded maladministration in general to be a constitutional basis for impeachment.

To think otherwise would make Madison an apologist for all the injustices and perversities that would grow out of unthinking adherence to the English common law and the practices of Parliament in pursuance or defiance of the unwritten constitution. On that score he put himself clearly on record in his protests against the Federalist contention of 1798–1800 that the Constitution by implication embodied the common law of England, and thereby conferred power on Congress to inflict punishments for all common-law crimes. Madison wrote in 1799:

"This doctrine, united with the assertion, that sedition is a common law offense, and therefore within the correcting power of Congress, opens at once the hideous volumes of penal law, and turns loose upon us the utmost invention of insatiable malice and ambition, which, in all ages, have debauched morals, depressed liberty, shackled religion, supported despotism, and deluged the scaffold with blood."

The Constitution again and again refers to impeachment in terms of criminal law: "to try," "convicted," "pardons for offenses . . . except impeachment," "conviction of treason," "bribery," "high crimes and misdemeanors," "trial of all crimes except . . . impeachment," "the party convicted." Not once is impeachment referred to in terms of civil law. The phrase "mere civil inquest," used more than once by House Managers to excuse impeachment attempts for noncriminal actions, is a perverted pickup from the British lecturer Wooddesson, who used the phrase "grand inquest of the nation" to explain the origin of the power of the House of Commons to move against the ministers of the king. "Grand inquest of the nation" implies high crimes by great and powerful criminals, highly protected; "mere civil inquest" bears the stamp of its own triviality, and consequently of its invalidity.

Treason, bribery, and other high crimes and high misdemeanors are the only constitutional grounds of impeachment, and this includes violation of the oath of office. Such violation, by criminal acts of commission or omission, is the only nonindictable offense for which the President, Vice President, judges, or other civil officers can be impeached.

But the history of impeachment in the United States shows all too plainly that House and Senate, if restrained only by their own sense of self-restraint, can twist "high crimes and misdemeanors" into an unrestricted power to impeach for any cause. The same can be done with violation of the oath of office. The necessity that lies ahead, therefore, is to search for an effective *restraint upon the power to misuse power.* That will be attempted in this book as it traces the history of impeachment.

CHAPTER 11

PLOT AND
COUNTERPLOT

THE FIRST IMPEACHMENT RESOLUTION adopted by the House
of Representatives was directed against a member of the
United States Senate. After investigating the charges, a
House committee headed by Samuel Sitgreaves of Massachusetts made this motion on July 5, 1797:

"Resolved, that William Blount, a Senator of the United
States, from the State of Tennessee, be impeached for high
crimes and misdemeanors."

Thus by implication, jurisdiction was based on Article
II, section 4, specifying the persons and offenses which come
under the impeachment provision. Taken up on July 7, the
motion at once led to the question whether members of
Congress were liable to impeachment. Chairman Sitgreaves
and his committee thought they were, and this view was
supported, Sitgreaves told the House, by Attorney General
Charles Lee and the eminent Philadelphia lawyers William
Rawle and William Lewis. Representatives John Nicholas
of Virginia and Albert Gallatin of Pennsylvania, a new-

comer to Congress, doubted this liability, but all parties agreed to go along with the action, thus throwing the decision onto the Senate. The resolution was adopted unanimously.

The facts were not open to question. On April 21, 1797, Senator Blount, former Commissioner of Southwestern Indian affairs (Cherokee and Creek), wrote to James Carey, government interpreter to the Cherokee tribe: "Among other things that I wished to have seen you about, was the business Captain Chesholm mentioned to the British Minister last winter at Philadelphia." Blount said he believed "the plan" would be attempted that fall, and "if the Indians act their part, I have no doubt but it will succeed." If the expected arrangements were made, "I shall myself have a hand in the business, and probably shall be at the head of the business on the part of the British."

No more was revealed concerning the plan, but Blount was emphatic about the groundwork to be laid. Above all, Carey must not let a word of it reach Benjamin Hawkins.* If possible, Carey should excite the Indians against Hawkins in order to secure his dismissal.

Blount closed with sound but self-convicting advice: "When you have read this letter three times, then burn it." Instead, Carey forwarded it to President Adams, who sent it to the House of Representatives for whatever action the House might choose to take. Thus Adams believed that senators were subject to impeachment.

Although Blount's plan was not disclosed in his letter, the debate on it brought out the facts. He had been plotting with England, which was at war with Spain, to mount an invasion of Spain's territory of Florida. The arrangement

---

* Blount's successor as Indian Commissioner. If Hawkins's high-minded principles had become permanent government policy, there would be no "Indian problem" in the United States today.

was that a filibustering expedition of Indians and frontiers-men, backed by a British fleet, would conquer Florida and establish British rule over that province and Louisiana. The conspiracy was known to the Spanish, who had been pro-testing to Washington about it for months. To cope with the invasion Spain and France were buying arms for ship-ment from Charleston to St. Augustine.

Interrogated, Blount admitted the authenticity of the letter. The committee found grounds for impeachment in Blount's "attempts to seduce Carey from his duty as a faith-ful interpreter," and to employ him as an engine to alienate the Indians. Under existing conditions, that did not fall far short of making war on the United States. In debate, however, emphasis was placed on what Gallatin described as "a conspiracy between a number of men, in the United States, and the British Government," involving an attack on Spain which, "if carried into effect, must involve us in a war with that nation."

Left undecided in the House action was the possible re-lationship between Blount's conduct and his official posi-tion. Clearly, he was not being impeached for actions as a senator, but his membership in the Senate magnified the international aspect of the plan if it had been carried into force. Chairman Sitgreaves, citing British precedent, sug-gested that Blount would be impeachable as a private Amer-ican citizen, even if exempt as a member of Congress, but he seemed less than enthusiastic about his own illustration. As the *Annals* record his speech:

"In England, Mr. Sitgreaves said, this trial by impeach-ment had been carried beyond official cases. He instanced the famous trial of Dr. [Henry] Sacheverell [1710], who was impeached for preaching a libellous sermon. It was well known that this cause divided the kingdom and that the first talents were called in to the aid of the Doctor."

The Senate swiftly added a new complication. On July 8, the day after the House voted to impeach, the Senate unanimously resolved that William Blount, "having been guilty of a high misdemeanor entirely inconsistent with his public trust and duty as a Senator, be, and he hereby is expelled from the Senate of the United States."

This compounded an already complicated case. Was a senator liable to impeachment? If so, did expulsion from the Senate end that liability? Or would expulsion leave him, as a private citizen, subject to impeachment regardless of his holding or not holding office, as he would have been under British law? Finally, if jurisdiction surmounted all these hurdles, did his attempt to organize a military expedition against Spain furnish valid grounds of impeachment?

The trial did not open until December 17, 1798—a year and a half after the House action. Five articles of impeachment charging "high misdemeanors" had been delivered to the Senate. Article I charged conspiracy to violate the declared neutrality of the United States in the Anglo-Spanish War by conspiring to organize and set on foot a hostile military expedition against Spanish territories on behalf of Great Britain. Article 2 accused Blount of violating the Spanish-American boundary treaty of 1795, under which "both parties oblige themselves expressly to restrain by force all hostilities on the part of the Indian nations living within their boundary." The remaining articles related to various aspects of Blount's attempt to "seduce" James Carey from the duty and trust of two government offices held by him. Of all these charges, the second was most clearly a high misdemeanor, since all treaties made by the United States are part of "the supreme law of the land." It was open to question, however, whether any of the offenses were indictable.

On March 1 the Senate voted a writ of summons commanding ex-Senator Blount to appear for trial on the third Monday in December. A plea by the House Managers for action in the current session was rejected—Congress might adjourn too soon for return of the writ.

This was all that happened on the surface; hidden from sight, however, was a struggle that converted Blount's trial from a simple decision on his fate into a contest over the liberties of the American people. On February 14 Senator Jacob Read of South Carolina had proposed the following motion:

"Resolved, that the duty or trust imposed by the Constitution of the United States, on a Senator of the United States, is not of such a nature as to render a Senator impeachable, or subject to any examination or trial for crimes or offenses alleged to have been committed against the laws and peace of the United States, *other than any citizen of the United States not a member of either House of Congress, and not holding an office under the said States.*" (Italics added.)

This wording asserted by implication that British impeachment practices were applicable in the United States, except for limitation of punishment. It meant that any American citizen could be impeached, tried, and by a vote of two thirds of the Senate, forever disqualified from holding any office under the United States.

On Read's initial claim of senatorial immunity from impeachment there was plenty of room for debate. The claim was obviously self-serving. One is tempted to ask what their decision would have been if the Constitution had empowered Congress to establish a pension system for "civil officers of the United States." Most likely, with skillful ratiocination, they would have decided that for certain purposes (pensions) they were civil officers, while for other purposes (impeachment) they were not.

Nor would such a distinction have been a totally disingenuous splitting of personality. During the framing of the Constitution, delegates discussing the impeachment of the President drew a distinction between his situation and that of the judiciary; also between the Executive and an elected legislature. Concerning the President, Madison remarked that limiting the period of his service was not sufficient security against incapacity, negligence, or perfidy: "The case of the Executive Magistracy was very distinguishable, from that of the Legislature or of any other public body, holding offices of limited duration. It could not be presumed that all or even a majority of an Assembly would either lose their capacity for discharging, or be bribed to betray, their trust." (July 20, 1787.)

Rufus King in the same debate saw no reason for subjecting any public servants to impeachment except those holding office during good behavior. As Madison's *Debates* were not published until 1840, senators could not resort to them in 1798 when the issue arose, but they needed no inferences drawn from the Federal Convention to prove themselves immune to impeachment as civil officers. The real significance and purpose of Senator Read's resolution lay in its implication that "any citizen of the United States not a member of either House of Congress, and not holding any office under the said States," could be impeached and permanently disqualified from holding any federal office, appointive *or elective.*

Vice President Jefferson realized the import and the menace of this Federalist maneuver. Sending the Read resolution to Madison, he said that the general lineup for it was 22 to 10, and observed:

"I see nothing in the mode of proceeding by impeachment but the most formidable weapon for the purpose of dominant faction that ever was contrived. It would be the most effectual one of getting rid of any man whom they may consider as dangerous to their views, and . . . history shows that in England impeachment has been an engine more of passion than of justice."

The Read resolution produced controversy even among the Federalists. It left senators open to impeachment, not as senators but as private citizens, if private citizens could be impeached. On motion of Theodore Sedgwick of Connecticut, a right-wing extremist, the resolution was referred to a committee "to report their opinion as to any amendment thereof (in point of form only), and at what time it will be proper to consider the subject thereof."

The purpose of amendment (Jefferson wrote to Madison the next day, February 22) was to make the exemption of senators absolute. The effect of the words "in point of form only" was to compel retention of the clause implying universal liability of private citizens to impeachment. Jefferson did not point this out, but he did say that it brought the claim into the light, with overwhelming support:

"Yesterday an opinion was declared that not only officers of the state governments, but every private citizen of the United States, are impeachable. Whether they will think this the time to make the declaration, I know not, but if they bring it on, I think there will not be more than two votes north of the Potomac against the universality of the impeaching power."

Madison replied on March 4:

"The universality of this power is the most extravagant novelty that has yet been broached, especially coming from a quarter that denies the impeachability of a Senator. Hardy as these innovators are, I cannot believe they will venture yet to hold this inconsistent and insulting language to the public. If the conduct and sentiments of the Senate on some occasions were to be regarded as the natural and permanent fruit of the institution, they ought to produce not only disgust, but despair, in all who are really attached to free government."*

The Read resolution never came to a vote. Presumably the Federalists thought it unwise to confront the American people with a declaration of the absolute immunity of senators from impeachment, coupled with the universal liability of private citizens to exclusion from office by that process. So the whole matter was passed along to the Senate sitting as a high court of impeachment, with the certainty that it would hold William Blount unimpeachable as a senator. The hope was that he would be convicted as a private citizen. Thus two objectives would be achieved at one seemingly natural stroke. Whatever the reasoning, the Blount impeachment trial was reduced at its outset to a single major question: Are all American citizens, regardless

---

*Professor W. W. Willoughby, in his three-volume commentaries on *The Constitution of the United States* (1929) made the astounding statement that "This doctrine [of universal liability to impeachment] was approved by Jefferson but repudiated by Madison." Willoughby gave a citation which explains his error: "See article entitled 'The Law of Impeachment in the United States,' by David Y. Thomas, in the *American Political Science Review*, May 1908. The author is much indebted to this valuable article." Willoughby would have been better off had he relied on his own research. Professor Thomas (of the University of Arkansas) quoted the following words, and no more, from Jefferson without comment: "I think that there will not be more than two votes north of the Potomac against the universality of the impeaching power." Willoughby construed this as an endorsement of universality. To anybody in the least familiar with Jefferson's opinion of Northern (i.e., Federalist) senators, his comment was akin to saying: "Every monarchist in the Senate will be for universality." Considering the modern worship of Jefferson and the universal resort of lawyers to Willoughby's *Commentaries*, his blunder is no trivial matter.

of official status, subject to impeachment, trial, and punishment by House and Senate?

If that thought appears incredible to Americans today, it fitted perfectly into the political conditions of 1798. The keys to it lie in the solitary penalty that could be inflicted upon a private citizen—perpetual exclusion from federal office—and in the proximity of the French Revolution.

In 1792, that three-year-old uprising for liberty had turned into a social war and blood bath. During the ensuing six years, American society became increasingly polarized between those who stood by the revolution in spite of its excesses, and those who viewed any expression of sympathy for it as the first stage of a similar uprising in the United States. Conservative American opinion followed opinion in England, where Thomas Paine fled the country to avoid prison for publishing *The Rights of Man*, and where the death penalty was imposed for advocating abolition of the "rotten borough" system of parliamentary apportionment.

War erupted between France and England, and tensions mounted in the United States. The Whisky Rebellion of 1794, brought on by discriminatory taxation of mountain farmers, led Alexander Hamilton to lament that its leaders could not be "compelled by outlawry to abandon their property, homes and the United States."

The newly formed Democratic Societies, falsely called revolutionary appendages of France, were threatened in that same year with what Madison termed " a vote of attainder" (which he defeated) in the House of Representatives.

The 1795 commercial treaty with England ("Jay's Treaty") made the United States a wartime economic ally of England against France. This provoked France to attack American ships and bred an American war spirit.

In 1796 the Presidential campaign was a contest, on the

hustings and in the press, between the "monarchist" John Adams and the "Jacobin traitor" Jefferson. The latter gained the Vice Presidency by being defeated for President. Then came President Adams's undeclared naval war with France, in which spontaneous bipartisan patriotic feelings were raised to fever pitch by the jingoistic messages and written addresses of the President to Federalist groups.

Into this cauldron of hate and fear, Congress in the spring of 1798 tossed a three-part program of political repression. It sought (1) to pass an Alien Act giving the President arbitrary power to expel all foreigners whom he considered "dangerous to the peace and safety of the United States," (2) to pass a Sedition Act subjecting all Americans (but especially newspaper editors) to prison terms for libeling the President and Congress, and (3) to make all American citizens liable to perpetual exclusion from office by expansive interpretation of the constitutional clauses on impeachment.

The Alien and Sedition Bills became acts of Congress, and lived and died in infamy. The impeachment maneuver failed and never found a place in American history. But these three monstrosities were triplets, conceived of the same Federalist parentage. The first was delivered in April, 1798, the second in July; the third was stillborn after six more months.

The same two congressmen who actively managed the Blount impeachment trial, James A. Bayard and Robert Goodloe Harper, were in the forefront of the drive for the Sedition Act. In the newspaper campaign for its passage, Federalist editors concentrated on Jefferson, Madison, and Gallatin as traitorous Americans who formed, they said, a counterpart of the Directory that ruled France after the fall of Robespierre. Jefferson, presiding over the Senate, saw clearly the peril to the country and the specific aim of the Sedition Act. On April 26, 1798, after the passage of the Alien Act and of a stiffened naturalization bill, he wrote to Madison:

"One of the war party, in a fit of unguarded passion, declared sometime ago they would pass a citizen[ship] bill, an alien bill, and a sedition bill. . . . There is now only wanting to accomplish the whole declaration before mentioned, a sedition bill, which we shall certainly soon see proposed. The object of that, is the suppression of the Whig presses. Bache's [Philadelphia *Aurora*] has been particularly named."

A month before, Jefferson had not been exaggerating when he wrote that if Senator Read's resolution implying power to impeach private citizens was put to the test, "there will not be more than two votes north of the Potomac against it." When the Sedition Bill came up in the Senate on July 4 (an appropriate day), 1798, exactly two votes from north of the Potomac were cast against it—one apiece from Maryland and New Hampshire. It was a striking symbol of the relationship between those two engines of repression.

When the Sedition Bill was taken up in the House on July 6, it was Robert Goodloe Harper, mastermind of the Blount impeachment, who shaped it for final passage. These are the words he wrote into the Senate version, to fortify its constitutional base:

"*Resolved,* that it is expedient to provide for the punishment, upon conviction in due form of law, of persons who shall write, print, utter, or publish, or cause to be written, printed, uttered or published . . . any false, scandalous, and malicious writing or writings against the Government of the United States, or either House of the Congress of the United States, or the President of the United States; with the intent to defame the said Government or either House of the said Congress, or the said President; or to bring them, or either of them into contempt or disrepute; or to excite against them, or any of them, the hatred of the good people of the United States; or to stir up sedition within the United States."

Harper's arguments in support of the bill were directed squarely against those whom he regarded as tools of France —men such as Jefferson, Madison, and Gallatin, although he did not name them. Opponents, he noted, were asking what changes had taken place in the country, since the peaceable adoption of the Constitution, to render such a law necessary. Harper's reply explained the purpose of the Blount trial as much as it did of the Sedition Bill:

"He did not know whether most to wonder at or pity the security of gentlemen who asked this question. . . . The change, in his opinion, consisted in this; that heretofore we had been at peace, and were now on the point of being driven into a war with a nation which openly boasts of its party among us, and its 'diplomatic skill' as the most effectual means of paralyzing our efforts, and bringing us to its own terms. Of the operations of this skill among us, by means of corrupt partisans and hired presses, he had no doubt; he was every day furnished with stronger reasons for believing in its existence, and saw stronger indications of its systematic exertion. . . .

"He knew no reason why we should not harbor traitors in our bosom as well as other nations, and he did most firmly believe that France had a party in this country; small, indeed, and sure to be disgraced and destroyed as soon as its design should become generally known, but active, artful, and determined, and capable, if it could remain concealed, of effecting infinite mischief. . . .

"To repress the enterprises of this party he wished for a law against seditions and libels, the two great instruments whereby France and her partisans had worked for the destruction of other countries, and he had no doubt were now working, he trusted unsuccessfully, for the destruction of this."

To ignore this menace, declared Harper, would be as foolish as the man who put on no coat of mail "when he saw the daggers of assassins everywhere whetted against him."

Every word Harper uttered in support of the Sedition Bill applied with equal force to his attempt to establish universal liability of citizens to impeachment, and to the universal scope of its constitutional grounds. When Blount's trial began in December 1798, his counsel, the eminent Philadelphia lawyers Alexander J. Dallas and Jared Ingersoll, lost no time in raising the question of liability.

Proceedings by impeachment, they asserted, were provided and permitted by the Constitution "only on charges of bribery, treason, and other high crimes and misdemeanors, alleged to have been committed by the President, Vice President, and other civil officers of the United States." They followed with a multiple denial of liability:

1. Blount "is *not now* a Senator."

2. As a Senator, he never was an *officer* of the United States.

3. He was not charged with having committed any crime or misdemeanor "in the execution of any civil office held under the United States." (That is, the offenses charged were unrelated to his senatorial duties.)

For these reasons, the attorneys asked whether the high court would have any further cognizance of the impeachment and whether Blount "ought to be compelled to answer." They wished to have this question decided first.

Their request not only served the interests of the defendant but coincided with the purposes of the prosecution. The Senate readily agreed, and the entire trial was devoted to arguing and answering the question of jurisdiction. Not a word was spoken about the plot to turn the Floridas and Louisiana over to Great Britain. The guilt or innocence of William Blount was reduced to insignificance; the issue at stake was the political rights of all Americans. Symbolically, they were on trial in the person of William Blount. His peril and theirs lay not in his liability or immunity from impeachment as a senator; that had been decided the preceding February in the 22 to 10 head count on the Read resolution. The vital question was the liability or immunity of a former senator who became a private citizen, not by resignation to escape trial, but by expulsion, and who thus, his counsel asserted, had the same status as any other private citizen. If he could be tried and convicted, any other American not holding office could be similarly impeached and punished.

That was exactly what the House Managers declared in their argument. Chairman James A. Bayard set forth two points:

1. "That all persons, without the supposed limitation [to President, Vice President, and civil officers of the United States] are liable to impeachment."

2. "That in order to carry into effect the general intent of the Constitution, a Senator must be considered as a civil officer."

The Managers placed all their emphasis upon the first point. The liability of senators to impeachment was argued last and perfunctorily, with full knowledge from prior debate in the Senate that it would be denied. In effect, the Senate casually disposed of senatorial liability as its final action in the trial, in order to leave full scope to the issue of universal liability to impeachment.

On that score Chairman Bayard declared that nowhere in the Constitution were "the cases defined, or the persons described, which were designed as the objects of impeachment." He took up the references to impeachment one by one, showing that some, and claiming that others, had no bearing on who could be impeached or for what reason. At last he came to Article II, section 4: "The President, Vice President, and all civil officers of the United States shall be removed from office on impeachment for and conviction of Treason, Bribery, or other high crimes and Misdemeanors." Identifying this only by its location—not daring to give its wording—he said it "provides that *certain officers* on conviction [of certain offenses] *shall be removed from office*." Nowhere in the Constitution, he declared with a straight face, "does an intention appear to declare *in what cases* an impeachment shall be sustained, or *to what persons* it shall be confined."

Many common terms, said Bayard, were used in the Constitution without definition—for example, "felony," "habeas corpus," "attainder," "privileges and immunities." The meaning of all such terms was "drawn from their import in the books of common law." So too it must be with "impeachment": The Constitution "has not described the persons who shall be the objects of impeachment, nor defined the cases to which the remedy shall be confined. We cannot do otherwise, therefore, than presume that upon these points, we are designedly left to the regulations of the common law." Having thus gutted the Constitution, Bayard said: "The question, therefore, is, what persons, for what offenses, are liable to be impeached at common law?" On this score he trusted that Mr. Blount's learned and liberal counsel would agree "that all of the King's subjects are liable to be impeached by the Commons, and tried by the Lords, upon charges of high crimes and misdemeanors." And to that extent go "the articles exhibited against William Blount." House Manager Harper reinforced Bayard's remarkable contention. The Constitution, Harper averred, was merely silent "as to the persons who shall be impeached besides the President, Vice President, and civil officers." Similarly, "as to the offenses for which they may be impeached, not a word is to be found in the Constitution." These matters were to be determined by the House of Representatives, to whom the "sole power of impeachment in all its latitude, and with all its properties and incidents, is given."

Having drawn this deduction from the alleged failure of the framers to say what they so clearly did say, Manager Harper laid down the rule for determining the scope of jurisdiction and of power:

"Where, then, Mr. President [The words were addressed to Vice President Jefferson, who was listening in silent horror] are we to look for those properties and incidents? Where shall we find the measure of this latitude? Not in the Constitution, surely, which says not one word on the subject; but in the common law of England, from whence the Constitution borrowed the term 'impeachment,' as it did so many other terms without explanation or restriction."

He continued:

"It cannot, then, I apprehend, be doubted that the term 'impeachment' in our Constitution has, and was intended by the framers of the Constitution to have, precisely the same meaning, force, and extent as in the English law. And it being perfectly clear that in the English law the power of impeachment is unlimited, and extends to every person and to every offense; it follows, undeniably, that the . . . defendant is liable to impeachment for the offenses charged against him by the House of Representatives."

Defense counsels Dallas and Ingersoll vigorously combated this "unexpected" line of argument—for which they had thoroughly prepared themselves. But instead of exposing and denouncing the partisan motives behind it, they met it with considered reasoning. The nearest they came to speaking the political truth was the opening intimation by Dallas that such an interpretation of the Constitution, extending the impeachment power "to every description of offender, and to every degree of offense," was entitled to respect only from the respectability of the Senate and the talents of the gentlemen who presented it. Said Dallas:

"A claim of jurisdiction so unlimited . . . ought surely to have been supported by an express and unequivocal delegation [of power]; but, behold, it rests entirely on an arbitrary implication from the use of a single word [impeachment]; and while the stream is thus copious, thus inundating, the source is enveloped (like the sources of the Nile) in mystery and doubt."

The Harper-Bayard doctrine, Dallas insisted, was contrary to the principles of our Federal compact, contrary to the general policy of the law of impeachments, "contrary to a fair construction of the very terms of the Constitution." To subject citizens in general to punishment by impeachment for any offense, he contended, would wipe out the demarcation between a national government of express and positive grants of power, and the residual powers left to the people and the states.

Dallas took up the claim that the grounds of impeachment set forth in the Constitution were "merely a recital, not to designate the objects of impeachment, but to point out a class of persons who, imperatively, *shall be removed from office* on impeachment for, and conviction of, treason, bribery, or other high crimes and misdemeanors." If that was merely a partial recital of powers, to which others could be added by implication, the same principle must be equally valid for the executive and judicial departments, "for the phraseology of the articles, with respect to the investment of their powers, is precisely the same." Surely, when it was provided that "the Judicial power of the United States shall be vested in one Supreme Court" and in inferior courts, "it was never thought that the power of the Federal Courts extended beyond the enumerated cases, though those cases are as much a matter of recital as the cases prescribed for the exercise of the impeachment power."

Dallas quoted Wooddesson's *Lectures* (2:596) on the origin and purpose of impeachment. It was certain, Wooddesson said, "that magistrates and officers entrusted with the administration of public affairs, may abuse their delegated powers to the extensive detriment of the community, and at the same time, in a manner not properly cognizable before the ordinary tribunals." Such delinquents were of great political influence. "The Commons, therefore, as the grand inquest of the nation, became suitors for penal justice," and both their own dignity and the safety of the accused required that they share this power with the Lords. "On this policy," Wooddesson concluded, "is founded the origin of impeachments, which began soon after the Constitution assumed its present form" (that is, soon after the "high court of Parliament" divided into Commons and Lords). All the king's subjects were impeachable in Parliament, wrote Wooddesson, because (as Dallas paraphrased him) "all subjects may be magistrates and public officers." But commoners could be convicted only of misdemeanors; they could be put to death only by *their* peers, not by *the* peers.

None of these intricacies of English law, Dallas contended, could be read by implication into the Constitution of the United States. The House of Commons in impeachment cases had at various times violated the British constitution. Was the United States to be bound by such violations? Or if the common law was to determine impeachable offenses, were the rules to be taken "from the dark and barbarous pages" of the ancient common law, or as the common law had been ameliorated by British statutory reform? Or would it be compiled as it had been differently modified in each of the American states that had adopted it? If so, how would the differences be harmonized? Was all this latitude, were all these properties and incidents of power, as Harper had called them, implied by the Constitution? Dallas declared:

"No, the words do not permit this latitude of jurisdiction, —the reason of the case does not require it. On the contrary, the Constitution presents a complete and consistent system;—it declares who shall impeach, who shall try, who may be impeached for what offenses, and how the delinquents shall be punished. Finding all these arrangements in the Constitution . . . it would be unjust and unreasonable to suppose the framers of that glorious document meant more than they have expressed, or left in doubt and ambiguity so important a part of their work. The power, as it relates to civil officers of the United States, is expressly given; it is not expressly given as relates to any other description of citizens; and, therefore, it is enough to observe, that it cannot be assumed as implied."

Dallas then proceeded to argue, though he had little need to do so, that elected members of Congress were not included under the term "civil officers," which was used merely to exempt military officers from impeachment in addition to removal by court martial. Had the framers intended to include senators and representatives, that intention would have been expressed.

Next Jared Ingersoll took up the impossible task of demonstrating that civil officers could be removed only for high crimes and misdemeanors *connected with their official functions*. On that score the word "treason" stared him in the face, and he lamely declared that treason in a President could not easily be dissociated from his office. Why, he asked, did the Constitution jump from treason to bribery, "a crime necessarily referring to the duties of office," if intermediate grades of crime unrelated to office were intended? The answer was hidden in Madison's *Notes of Debates*. The clause, before its expansion, specified only treason and bribery; then when "other high crimes and misdemeanors" were added, bribery was left in merely because it was already there.

Bayard made mincemeat of Ingersoll—and also of himself—in his reply. "There is not a syllable in the Constitution," he said truthfully, "which confines impeachment to official acts"; and to do so "is against the plain dictates of common sense." But instead of citing rape, murder, or some such manifest grounds of removal for high crimes, he laid bare the inmost purposes of the Blount trial by saying:

"Let us suppose that a Judge of the United States, forgetting his duty and the gravity of his situation, instead of using his authority in case of an insurrection, to quell the insurgents, should aid them in their violence. Surely this would not be an official act; and shall I be told, for that reason, that he shall not be liable to impeachment? How else is he to be removed?"

This illustration linked the Blount trial with the devastating assault on democratic self-government then being made by the Federalist Party. Harper, Bayard, and the Federalist senators had insurrections on the brain.

To grasp the full political import of this remark about aid to insurrections, one must go back to Bayard's main speech affirming the universal power of impeachment. Answering the argument that such a proceeding would be unsuitable because of the limited punishment which could be inflicted upon private citizens (perpetual disqualification to hold office), Bayard said that in some cases this punishment "would be the most suitable which could be inflicted."

What must have been the thoughts of Vice President Thomas Jefferson, who as a candidate for President in 1796 had been called a tool of France and a conspirator against his country by virtually every Federalist editor in the nation, as he watched the painting of a Federalist portrait of himself by the chairman of the House Managers? Said Bayard:

"Let us suppose, that a citizen not in office, but possessed of extensive influence, arising from popular arts, from wealth or connexions, actuated by strong ambition, and aspiring to the first place in the Government, should conspire with the disaffected of our own country, or with foreign intriguers, by illegal artifice, corruption, or force, to place himself in the Presidential chair. I would ask, in such a case, what punishment would be more likely to quell a spirit of that description, than absolute and perpetual disqualification for any office of trust, honor, or profit under the Government, and what punishment could be better calculated to secure the peace and safety of the State from the repetition of the same offense?"

Here was a clear revelation of Federalist Party strategy: to control the Presidential election of 1800 by combining impeachment with the Sedition Act. Republican (Democratic) editors were to be silenced by prosecution for seditious libel, while party candidates were menaced with impeachment either as officeholders or as private citizens. Vice President Jefferson could be brought in by the Bayard-Harper expansion of the grounds of removal, and could not escape impeachment by resigning. Madison, who had retired from Congress, could be impeached as a private citizen. Jefferson's Kentucky Resolutions and Madison's Virginia Resolutions of 1798 both were designed to overthrow the

Sedition Act, making their sponsors perfect targets for a rule of universal liability to impeachment for any cause.

The plan failed, obviously because a count of heads in the strongly Federalist Senate showed that fewer than two thirds were brave enough to go through with it. A vote on universal liability was avoided because defeat would tend to foreclose a future attempt. So the trial of William Blount ended with a simple finding that senators could not be impeached—a verdict that could have been given in February 1798, without any trial at all, by passage of Senator Read's resolution affirming their exemption.

No part of this extraordinary record of political intrigue and chicanery has come down into present-day discussions of the constitutional power and purposes of impeachment. The Blount trial, intended as an adjunct to the Sedition Act of 1798, has been ignored or glossed over by historians and soberly presented by later House Managers of impeachment as an honest attempt by disinterested, high-minded early statesmen to fathom the intentions of the framers of the Constitution. They went too far, the consensus is, in following British precedent into universal liability; but the failure of subsequent researchers to pierce their motives has helped to establish grounds of removal that violate the Constitution. Although they failed in their own endeavor, they succeeded in corrupting impeachment proceedings in all later periods. Their precedent has gained force as it receded in time, and it has never been stronger than in the last half century.

CHAPTER III

ALCOHOLISM IN
A FEDERALIST JUDGE

THE SEDITION ACT OF 1798, combined with the Federalist Party's monopoly of the national judiciary, had a great influence upon President Jefferson's attitudes toward the impeachment of judges. One of his earliest actions after taking office in 1801 was to free all editors, publishers, letter writers, and lawyers who were still in prison as violators of that law. The act's first victim, Congressman Matthew Lyon of Vermont, who had been triumphantly reelected while in jail, already was free through expiration of his sentence. His "crime" had been to write that the devotion of President Adams to public welfare was "swallowed up in a continual grasp for power, in an unbounded thirst for ridiculous pomp, foolish adulation, and selfish avarice." Lyon received a year in prison for that, with a framer of the Constitution, Supreme Court Justice William Paterson, presiding over his trial.

Partly to strengthen the Federalist hold on the judiciary,

the Sixth Congress in its dying hours had passed a bill creating sixteen new federal judgeships, to form a much
needed circuit court system, and added a batch of justices
of the peace. The maneuver reflected Federalist fear that
the incoming Republican administration, unless restrained
by the judiciary, would send Federalist leaders to prison in
retaliation for their misuse of the Sedition Act. They would
be safe, they felt, if they could control the courts for four
years, which would be sufficient time for the American
people to return to their senses and restore the government
to those who were born to rule. ("Qualified" was the
Federalist word.)

The law was passed, the "midnight judges" were nominated and confirmed, their commissions were made out, and
some were delivered—all in a day. Several justice of the
peace commissions, however, were lying on the desk of the
Secretary of State when the Jefferson administration took
over. The President ordered them withheld and asked
Congress to repeal the new judiciary act which had established sixteen circuit judgeships.

The Federalists were thrown into panicky fury. The bill
was unconstitutional, they said; it violated the provision on
tenure; the Supreme Court would declare it unconstitutional. This idea gave them new cause for fright: all members of the Court would be impeached. The Republicans,
Representative James A. Bayard predicted, were about "to
give notice to the judges of the Supreme Court of their
fate, and to bid them to prepare for their end." Bayard
justified his party's past course in a sentence: They had been
forced into it because "the wild principles of French liberty
were scattered through the country."

The judiciary act was repealed, the new circuit judgeships were abolished, and a mandamus proceeding entitled

Marbury v. *Madison* was begun in the Supreme Court to compel the Secretary of State to deliver one of the withheld justice of the peace commissions.

Talk of wholesale impeachments was consequently in the air when the Jefferson administration found sufficient cause of action against Judge John Pickering of the New Hampshire district, who was making a daily spectacle of himself on the bench because of intoxication aggravated by copious and blasphemous profanity. Compounding his offense came allegations of his misconduct in an admiralty case late in 1802. This, however, was mere window dressing: the legal irregularities were an evident by-product of intoxication.

All the force of the administration lay behind the articles of impeachment sent by the House to the Senate on March 3, 1803, the day on which that Congress expired. When the case came to trial a year later, party passions ran far deeper than the specific issues, which were two: Was chronic intoxication on the bench a "high misdemeanor"? And were the admiralty proceedings impeachable? (They should have been resolved by appeal.) The real question in all minds was whether the Federalists could hold the judiciary intact against selective removals or whether the Jeffersonians would be able to breach the Federalist judicial monopoly.

The action was begun "in the name of the House of Representatives, and of all the people of the United States." That, as in the House of Commons, was meant to dignify the function of the House of Representatives as "the grand inquest of the nation." The first three articles dealt with the admiralty case. The fourth alleged that "the said John Pickering being a man of loose morals and intemperate habits," did on November 11, 1802, "appear on the bench of the said court for the purpose of administering justice, in a state of total intoxication . . . and did then and there frequently, in a most profane and indecent manner, invoke the name of the Supreme Deity . . . and was then and there guilty of other high misdemeanors."

Judge Pickering did not appear before the Senate, nor was he represented by counsel. Instead, Federalist senators conducted his defense, while Jeffersonian senators were more active in the prosecution than the House Managers, who merely presented evidence of Pickering's conduct. The judge's son, Jacob S. Pickering, laid the groundwork for the defense in a petition presented at the opening of the trial. In it he declared that his father, at the time of the alleged crimes and for more than two years before, was "and now is insane, his mind wholly deranged." Consequently, the son averred, "the said John Pickering is incapable of corruption of judgment, not subject of impeachment, or amenable to any tribunal for his actions . . . and his disorder has baffled all medical aid."

Substitute "mental illness" for "insanity" and this plea forecasts the mid-twentieth-century shift in the classification of alcoholism, from an indictable misdemeanor to a disease calling for medical treatment. But since the Constitution failed to make "incapacity" a ground of impeachment, there were only two ways of getting Pickering off the court. The Senate either had to classify habitual drunkenness on the bench as an impeachable misdemeanor, or expand the grounds of removal beyond "high crimes and misdemeanors." To make the first course more difficult, Jacob Pickering assured the Senate in his petition that until his father suffered this most deplorable of calamities, "the loss of reason, he was unexceptionable in his morals, remarkable for the purity of his language, and the correctness of his habits." The deviations from this conduct "now complained of, are irresistible evidence of the deranged state of his mind."

Senatorial supporters of the judge at once called for an

investigation to determine whether Pickering was or was not insane at the time of his misconduct. Jeffersonian Senators resisted; they saw a plain case of drunken misbehavior. The Managers, said Congressman Peter Early of Georgia, "have charged him with acts highly derogatory to his character as a man; with transgressions disgraceful to him as a judge; with crimes ruinous to the interest and reputation of his Government." The Senate should act.

Pushing the insanity defense, Federalist senators made one motion after another, changing the form as each was voted down. Under the rules adopted for the trial, all votes had to be taken in open session; all debate had to be held behind closed doors. For two days the little Senate gallery was opened and closed with regularity as crowds of visitors were shuttled in and out. Senatorial tempers flared.

On March 10, the third day of the trial, Senator White of Delaware, a leading Federalist, offered one more resolution: "That this court is not at present prepared to give their final decision" upon the articles of impeachment, for the reason that no inquiry had been made into the suggestion that the judge had failed to appear before the court because he "was and yet is insane."

To the majority, this was an accusation that they were attempting to conduct an *ex parte* prosecution (as indeed they were). Senator Wilson Cary Nicholas of Virginia, head spokesman for President Jefferson, exclaimed that such a motion should "not be permitted to go upon the journals of the court." Senator William Jackson of Georgia, another administration man, moved the previous question, calling for an immediate vote upon the motion.

Under customary practice the motion for the previous question was usually made by somebody opposed to the matter before the house, who would then vote against his own motion for the purpose of postponing action on the main subject. Here, however, the purpose was to prevent debate upon it, as shown by an entry in Senator John Quincy Adams's diary:

"On this resolution it was not without the utmost difficulty that any discussion whatsoever could be obtained."

Adams told of Senator Nicholas's maneuver against the resolution and continued: "The next struggle was to prevent all debate upon the resolution. By our rules there can be no debate on any motion in open court. A motion to close the doors for the purpose of discussing the resolution was rejected."

Rejection of the motion to close the doors, which lost by one vote, was in effect a refusal to allow any debate on White's resolution and a mandate for immediate action on the motion for the previous question. However, a question put by Republican Senator John Smith of Ohio changed the situation. He wanted to know the purpose of the White resolution. "The answer," Adams recorded in his diary, "could not be given in public so he [Smith] reversed his position and furnished the additional vote needed to go into conclave."* Adams continued:

"The galleries were cleared, and a short discussion of the resolution was held . . . Mr. Anderson [of Tennessee] and most of the Members of the majority all the time manifesting the most extreme impatience to open the doors and stop all further debate."

The violence of the discussion culminated in an offer to fight a duel. Senator William Maclay of Pennsylvania de-

---

*White's motion was offered, Senator Adams made clear, because both sides recognized that impeachment required proof of criminal conduct. The Jeffersonians endeavored to exclude evidence that Pickering was insane "only from the fear, that if insanity should be proved, he cannot be convicted of high crimes and misdemeanors by acts of decisive madness." (1 Memoirs, 299–300.)

scribed the scene in his diary: "Mr. Nicholas vociferated order, order, order—I will not submit to hear our proceedings called by the degrading name of a mock trial."

To which Senator White replied that he did not intend to offend the Virginia senator, but he would not retract those words. "If in this I have offended him, I am willing and ready to give him satisfaction at any time and place he will please to name."

A motion to open the doors carried, creating the same effect as if Senator Jackson's motion for the previous question had been put and carried. It cut off debate, and the White resolution was put to an immediate vote and defeated, 19 to 9.* It is obvious that no such acrimony could have been stirred by the mere issue of chronic drunkenness as a ground of impeachment, or by the justice or injustice that was being meted out to an unfortunate district judge. At the bottom were the determination of the Federalist Party to hold onto the judiciary and the resolve of the Republican Party to break that hold. The Federalists were now demanding the fairness they had refused to grant in the trial of Senator Blount, and the Republicans were likewise reversing themselves.

In his next maneuver, Senator White moved that in determining guilt or innocence, the question be put in a form which, he said, was nearly the same as in the celebrated British case of Warren Hastings: "Is John Pickering, district judge of the district of New Hampshire, guilty of high crimes and misdemeanors upon the charges contained in

---

*For a more extended account of this early restriction of debate in the Senate (which defenders of the filibuster say never occurred until modern times) see Irving Brant, "Memorandum on the Development of Cloture and the Previous Question in American and British Practice," placed by Senator Paul G. Douglas of Illinois in the *Congressional Record*, May 9, 1957 (pp. 5961–5), and republished in the *Record* of January 5, 1961.

the ———— article of impeachment or not guilty?"

This was embarrassing to the Jeffersonians. Some of them, it appeared, were ready to vote Judge Pickering off the bench, but balked at labeling his conduct "high crimes and misdemeanors." Senator Joseph Anderson of Tennessee proposed another wording: "Is John Pickering, district judge of the district of New Hampshire, *guilty as charged* in the ———— article of impeachment exhibited against him by the House of Representatives?"

This form was adopted 18 to 9—an exact two-thirds majority, which pointed toward removal; but it threw the proceedings wide open to attack for lack of candor. Also, it raised a basic question concerning constitutional grounds of impeachment.

Since all debate had to be secret, the galleries once more were cleared and Senator White took the floor. He believed that Judge Pickering "had practiced much of the indecent and improper conduct charged against him." But White was "very far from believing that any part of his conduct amounted to high crimes and misdemeanors," because there was scarcely a doubt "but that the judge was actually insane at the time."

What was the significance, White wanted to know, of the shift in the form of the question placed before the Senate? Did the change of wording mean that the Senate intended "only to find the facts, and to avoid pronouncing the law upon them"? Could they have it in view to say "merely, that Judge Pickering had committed the particular acts charged against him in the articles of impeachment, and, upon such a conviction, to remove him, without saying directly or indirectly whether these acts amounted to high crimes and misdemeanors or not"?

White then got down to the bedrock issue: tenure "during good behavior" or tenure during the "pleasure of the

Senate," which the framers thought they had forbidden when they inserted the requirement of "high crimes and misdemeanors." He said of the majority wording:

"Upon such a principle, and by such a mode of proceeding, *good behavior would no longer be the tenure of office;* every officer of the Government must be *at the mercy of a majority of Congress,* and it will not hereafter be necessary that a man should be guilty of high crimes and misdemeanors in order to render him liable to removal from office by impeachment, but a conviction upon any facts stated in articles exhibited against him will be sufficient."

That description can truthfully be applied to the position of the House Managers in virtually every impeachment from 1797 down to the present day. Senator White could have stated the case even more strongly: he could have said that the adopted procedure violated the sacrosanct clause declaring, "The Senate shall have the sole power to try all impeachments." If the House had power to present a set of facts as impeachable, and the Senate found the facts to be true and removed Pickering for them, at the same time refusing to declare the facts to be constitutional grounds of impeachment, the most important portion of the trial would be turned over to the House of Representatives.

Senator Jonathan Dayton of New Jersey, who had been the youngest delegate to the Philadelphia Convention of 1787 and was now a Federalist gut-fighter, reinforced White's argument and carried the debate into personalities. The Senate, he remarked, "were now to be compelled, by a determined majority, to take the question in a manner never before heard of on similar occasions. They were simply to be allowed to vote whether Judge Pickering was guilty as charged—that is, guilty of the facts charged in each article—aye or no. If voted guilty of the facts, the sentence was to follow, without any previous question whether those facts amounted to a high crime and misdemeanor." Dayton turned to the underlying motive:

"The latent reason of this course was too obvious. There were numbers who were disposed to give sentence of removal against this unhappy judge, upon the ground of the facts alleged and proved, who could not, however, conscientiously vote that they amounted to high crimes and misdemeanors, especially when committed by a man proved at the very time to be insane, and to have been so ever since, even to the present moment. The Constitution gave no power to the Senate, as the High Court of Impeachments, to pass such a sentence of removal and disqualification, except upon charges and conviction of high crimes and misdemeanors."

The House Managers, Dayton observed, had charged that Judge Pickering was guilty of such crimes, and had exhibited articles and evidence in support of the charges. The Senate had heard the evidence and gone through certain forms of a trial. "They now, by a majority, dictate the form of a final question, the most extraordinary, unprecedented, and unwarrantable." For himself, Dayton said, "he was free to declare that he believed the respondent guilty of most of the facts stated in the articles, but considering the deranged state of intellect of that unfortunate man, he could not declare him guilty in the words of the Constitution; he could not vote it a conviction under the impeachment."

Dayton then said he would not object to a preliminary question, "whether guilty of the facts charged in each article," provided the Senate would allow it to be followed by another most important question: "Whether those facts, thus proved and found, amounted to a conviction of high crimes and misdemeanors, as charged in the impeachment, and expressly required by the Constitution." Senator White immediately phrased just such a question and asked the president *pro tem* to rule on it.

The ruling was that such a motion could not be received after the preliminary question had been voted on. This decision, of course, made the preliminary question a final one if it was voted on, and stamped the whole proceeding even more decisively as an evasion of the terms of the Constitution. Senator Wright of Maryland embroidered on the evasion by proposing that the question of "guilty as charged" be followed by another:

"Is the Court of opinion that John Pickering be removed from the office of judge of the district court of the district of New Hampshire?"

At this point Senators John Armstrong of New York, Stephen R. Bradley of Vermont, David Stone of North Carolina, together with Dayton and White, "retired from the Court." The last two stated their reason: The motion prevented them from giving their opinion on the insanity of Pickering and on the question whether the charges in the articles of impeachment "amounted in him to high crimes and misdemeanors or not."

The Senate then by a vote of 19 to 7 found Judge Pickering "guilty as charged in the first article of impeachment." The same division occurred on the three other articles, and one more vote was picked up on the final question. The Senate declared itself 20 to 6 of "opinion that John Pickering be removed from the office of judge" of the New Hampshire district court. And by that opinion he was removed without a finding that his conduct afforded constitutional grounds of removal; indeed, without a formal "hereby is removed."

Three of the five senators who walked out were Republicans. Presumably they disapproved of the impeachment but were unwilling to rebuke President Jefferson by voting for acquittal. Or possibly they regarded Judge Pickering as unfit to continue in office but wanted no active part in his removal by this dubious procedure. Dayton and White, the Federalists who walked out, had helped fasten the Sedition Act on the country. Their boycott was plainly a slap at the President and did not affect the result. However, if all five had remained in the chamber and voted in accordance with their beliefs, Pickering would have kept his seat by a one-vote margin. Their absence, combined with the votes of the Jeffersonian majority, inflicted a blot upon the Senate and helped to pervert the Constitution.

CHAPTER IV

THE TRIAL
OF SAMUEL CHASE

JUDGE PICKERING HAVING BEEN SCALPED, the Jefferson administration turned to bigger game. Thanks to President Adams's appointment of John Marshall as Chief Justice and Bushrod Washington (nephew of George) as associate justice, the Supreme Court no longer formed a solid phalanx of sedition exterminators. However, nearly all the men who had ruthlessly enforced the Sedition Act were still on the bench, and its entire membership was of the Federalist stripe. Among the justices, none was so widely hated as Samuel Chase of Maryland, whose high legal attainments were eclipsed by his bias and vindictiveness in political prosecutions on the circuit bench.

During the American Revolution Chase had been an ardent patriot and nationalist. "America has now taken her rank among the nations!" he jubilantly exclaimed when he heard of the 1778 treaty of alliance with France. He was also an avid purchaser of confiscated British property sold by the state and paid for in depreciated state currency. As the head of Maryland's "paper money party," he fought against the Constitution because it forbade the states to issue bills of credit. As a justice of the Supreme Court, however, his most notable opinion was in *Ware* v. *Hylton* (1796), a landmark in nationalism. By virtue of the 1783 treaty of peace, the Court in this case upheld the power of the United States to nullify Virginia's confiscation act of 1777—a law similar to the Maryland law from which Chase had reaped a fortune.

At an early period of his judicial tenure also, Justice Chase ruled that the common law of England was not embodied by implication in the Constitution of the United States, and that common-law crimes therefore could not be punished by federal judges in the absence of federal statutes. All his Supreme Court colleagues who had that question brought before them in circuit court made a contrary ruling, which the Marshall Court ultimately overthrew, holding that there was no such thing as a Federal common law.

From his own judicial past and his proven talents, Chase ought to have been a mainstay of constitutional rights during the madness inspired by the French Revolution and the rise of egalitarian American democracy. Instead, he turned Federalist and was swept away by the frenzy of the period, during which his strong personality and misapplied legal learning made him the foremost symbol of judicial tyranny. "A licentious press," Chase wrote in 1796, "is the bane of freedom." The press was licentious when it called President Adams an arrogant monarchist; it was exercising its freedom when it characterized Vice President Jefferson as a servile traitor in the pay of France. Chase acted in accord with his principles, preserving freedom by suppressing it in the opposition party.

Undeniably, Justice Chase had made himself unfit for his position. Under obvious pressure from President Jefferson, the House of Representatives began impeachment proceedings late in 1804. There are indications that Jefferson, whose devotion to freedom of expression was considerably more consistent in the abstract than the concrete, was moved to this course by the successful impeachment of a state judge, Alexander Addison, by the Pennsylvania legislature in 1803. Governor Thomas McKean of Pennsylvania wrote to the President that Addison had been "the transmontane Goliath of federalism in this state, a remarkable political apostate, and in my opinion federalism will fall with him in the six western counties. . . . So you find sir we know how to get rid of obnoxious judges as well as the Congress." (February 7, 1804.)

Governor McKean said that he had it in mind to check "the infamous and seditious libels published almost daily in our Pennsylvania newspapers." This could be done, he thought, by a few prosecutions for criminal libel, but as the President and Congress were the most frequent objects of this abuse, he wanted Presidential advice and consent before going ahead. Jefferson replied that the Federalist press was "pushing its licentiousness and its lying to such a degree of prostitution as to deprive it of all credit." He had long thought that a few libel actions would help to restore integrity, but they should be brought under state law and without any "general prosecution, for that would look like persecution."

Coming just after the impeachment of Judge Pickering (but before his trial), this exchange was a natural prelude to the move against Justice Chase, whose impeachment for "high crimes and misdemeanors" was sent to the Senate in December 1804. The first article dealt with Chase's conduct in the treason prosecution of John Fries, a farmer-auctioneer of German parentage and a veteran of the Revolutionary War. Fries organized the Pennsylvania Dutch farmers of his county in armed resistance to the 1798 "war taxes" aimed at France. The violence was microscopic, but the United States Army was called out by President Adams. The farmers went home, and Fries went into hiding. His only remaining follower was a dog named Whisky who, reversing the ordinary pattern of alcoholic addiction, could not get along without Fries. So Whisky followed Fries, the army followed Whisky, and the farmer-auctioneer was haled into federal court. Justice Chase demanded and obtained a grand jury indictment accusing him of treason. Fries was tried by Chase, found guilty, and sentenced to death.

The charge of treason was preposterous. On a comparative basis Daniel Shays, leader of Shays' Rebellion of 1787, ought to have been hanged, drawn, and quartered; yet he escaped trial altogether by leading his party to victory in the next Massachusetts state election. Of course, the auctioneer's eloquence of John Fries was in the German tongue and did not carry beyond his home county. But the exaggerated charge of treason and the cruel sentence stirred even Federalist leaders to protest, and President Adams averted national disgrace by giving Fries a pardon.

Six years later the justice who tried and sentenced Fries was himself placed on trial, not as the result of lasting indignation over repeated injustice, but as a calculated maneuver to create a vacancy on the Supreme Court. The first article specified that Chase in the treason trial of John Fries "did in his judicial capacity, conduct himself in a manner highly arbitrary, oppressive, and unjust." To wit:

1. He delivered an opinion in writing on the material question of law "tending to prejudice the minds of the jury . . . before counsel had been heard in their defense."

2. He restricted Fries's counsel from citing English authorities on the nature of treason.

3. He debarred Fries's counsel (and thereby debarred

Fries) from the constitutional privilege of addressing the jury "on the law as well as on the fact, which was to determine his guilt or innocence."

This meant that the lawyers were forbidden to argue that Chase had misconstrued the Constitution. Upon this ruling Fries's attorneys abandoned the defense and left the courtroom.

The next five articles of impeachment dealt with Chase's conduct in presiding over the trial of James T. Callender, a Virginia printer indicted under the Sedition Act. His sedition consisted of writing during the electoral campaign of 1800: "Take your choice, then, between Adams, war and beggary, and Jefferson, peace and competency."

The House of Representatives charged that Chase, with intent to secure Callender's conviction, refused to dismiss juryman John Bassett, "who wished to be excused . . . because he had made up his mind" against the defendant. It was charged also that Chase improperly excluded a witness for Callender, denied bail contrary to law, and exhibited conduct "marked, during the whole course of the said trial, by manifest injustice, partiality, and intemperance." This included "unusual, rude and contemptuous expressions toward the prisoner's counsel," causing them to retire from the Court. In sum, Chase manifested an indecent solicitude "for the conviction of the accused, unbecoming even a public prosecutor, but highly disgraceful to the character of a judge, as it was subversive of justice."

Article 7 declared that Chase refused to discharge a Delaware grand jury which ignored his statement "that a highly seditious temper had manifested itself in the State of Delaware, among a certain class of people . . . more especially . . . in Wilmington where lived a most seditious printer" (that is, the publisher of the *Mirror of the Times and General Advertiser*).

Article 8 accused the justice of delivering to the Maryland circuit court grand jury "an intemperate and inflammatory political harangue, with intent to excite the fears and resentment of the said grand jury, and of the good people of Maryland, against their state government and constitution; and . . . against the Government of the United States." Even if Chase were competent as a judge to express such opinions, they "were at the time, and as delivered by him, highly indecent, extra-judicial, and tending to prostitute the high judicial character with which he was invested, to the low purpose of an electioneering partizan."

These articles presented a partisanly worded but accurate description of Chase's conduct on the occasions described. A judge who acted as he did ought not to be on the bench; but had he committed any "high crimes and misdemeanors" to warrant removal by impeachment? Not, certainly, if it was necessary to prove that evil purpose had motivated his actions. Chase was as ardent a patriot in 1798 as he had been in 1776; it was just that in the later period he was saving his country from the imagined dangers of a transplanted French Revolution and the iniquities of American democracy.

Chairman of the House Managers was John Randolph of Virginia, preeminent for shrill-voiced oratorical wizardry, a violent temper, long legs, big feet, and a bigger ego. Still one year away from being deposed as administration spokesman in the House, his influence was high in that body but correspondingly low in the Senate. It was not improved, according to Jeffersonian Senator William Cocke of Tennessee, by his boasts that he was going to wipe the floor with the obnoxious justice. Associate Managers included George W. Campbell of Tennessee, later senator and Secretary of the Treasury; Caesar Rodney of Delaware, who became Jefferson's Attorney General; Joseph H. Nicholson of

Philadelphia, who stepped into a federal judgeship, and Peter Early of Georgia, a native of Virginia.

Chase was defended by a formidable battery of lawyers, including Robert Goodloe Harper, who as a member of the House had been one of the Managers of the impeachment trial of Senator Blount. Equally notable was Luther Martin, attorney general of Maryland for the previous twenty-seven years. His oratorical reputation packed the United States Supreme Court's little auditorium whenever he took part in a case. With these two were the distinguished Joseph Hopkinson of the Philadelphia bar, and Washington's last Attorney General, Charles Lee, who in 1797 had attempted to prosecute Congressman Samuel J. Cabell for sedition but had been routed by the verbal barrage of the Virginia legislature.

Justice Chase appeared in person before the Senate on January 2, 1805, and read a paper in which he maintained:

"To these articles . . . I say that I have committed no crime or misdemeanor whatsoever for which I am subject to impeachment according to the Constitution of the United States. I deny, with a few exceptions, the acts with which I am charged; I shall contend, that all acts admitted to have been done by me were *legal*, and I deny, in every instance, the *improper* intentions with which the acts charged are alleged to have been done, and in which their supposed criminality altogether consists."

Since the whole question was one of motives, the House Managers dwelt on that aspect when the trial opened in February. The testimony of John Thompson Mason was typical: Concerning the pressure by Chase for indictment of James Callender, Mason related that before the justice left Richmond, he said he would "teach the people to distinguish between the liberty and the licentiousness of the press . . . that if the Commonwealth or its inhabitants were not too depraved to furnish a jury of good and respectable men, he would certainly punish Callender."

Item by item Randolph built up the case, proving by witnesses that Chase did or said nearly all the things described in the charges. Manager Early summed up the case with oratorical fervor:

"He stands charged with violating the sacred charter of our liberties, and with setting at naught the most holy obligations of society. He stands charged with perverting the high judicial functions of his office for the purposes of individual oppression, and of staining the pure ermine of justice by political party spirit."

Quite so; but with what recognizable "high crimes and misdemeanors" was he charged? Manager Campbell undertook to eliminate that element as unnecessary for conviction. Removal from office and disqualification for future office, said he, "cannot be considered a criminal punishment; it is merely a deprivation of rights." By setting up this limitation, the Constitution evidently meant to leave punishment for actual crimes to courts of ordinary jurisdiction:

"Impeachment, therefore, according to the meaning of the Constitution, may fairly be considered a kind of inquest into the conduct of an officer, merely as it regards his office; the manner in which he performs the duties thereof; and the effects that his conduct therein may have on society. It is more in the nature of a civil investigation than of a criminal prosecution."

Even treason and bribery, Campbell contended, were only impeachable so far as they "may be considered as a violation of the duties of the officer" and of his oath to support the Constitution and laws of the United States. The criminality of treason and bribery, independent of the office, "must be inquired into and punished by indictment."

This construction, he said, was absolutely necessary to avoid the absurdity of punishing a man twice for the same offense.

"Hence I conceive [Campbell concluded] that in order to support these articles of impeachment, we are not bound to make out such a case as would be punishable by indictment in a court of law. It is sufficient to show that the accused has transgressed the line of his official duty, in violation of the laws of his country; and that this conduct can only be accounted for on the ground of impure and corrupt motives."

Examination of the evidence, Campbell told the Senate, would make it clear that the judge had displayed "a corrupt partiality and predetermination unjustly to oppress" those who differed from him in political sentiments. This had resulted in "turning the judicial power, with which he was vested, into an engine of political oppression."

Campbell's argument was a disaster for the prosecution. Aware that Justice Chase had violated no positive law, he not only reduced impeachment to a mere inquiry into general fitness for office, but treated the specific crimes mentioned in the Constitution—treason and bribery—as nonimpeachable unless the overt acts were connected with the duties of office. Yet while denying the need to prove indictable criminality, he conceded that misconduct, to warrant impeachment, must violate the laws of the country and must grow out of "impure and corrupt motives," of which there was not the slightest evidence. To get still farther away from the need for proving criminality, he actually gave persons impeached for "high crimes and misdemeanors" the protection against double jeopardy—ignoring the express words of the Constitution that "the party convicted shall, nevertheless, be liable and subject to indictment, trial, judgment, and punishment according to law."

Defense counsel Joseph Hopkinson lost no time in pointing this out, and took an extreme position on the other side: "I offer it as a position I shall rely upon in my argument, that no judge can be impeached and removed from office for any act or offense for which he could not be indicted. It must be by law an indictable offense." The evil of double jeopardy was prevented by the limitation of punishment in cases of impeachment to removal from office and future disqualification.

While saying that impeachment would lie only for an indictable offense, Hopkinson rejected the converse of the proposition. Not all indictable offenses, he declared, furnished ground for impeachment. "Far from it. A man may be indictable for many violations of positive law which evince no *mala mens,* no corrupt heart or intention, but which would not be the ground of an impeachment." He gave an illustration: ordinary assault; then emphasized that the word "high" in the Constitution applied equally to "crimes and to misdemeanors."

If nothing was impeachable that was not indictable, for what acts might a man be indicted? Must action not be based "on some known law of the society in which he resides?" Any act, said Hopkinson, "which is *contra bonos mores* is indictable as such," under the general protection which the common law "gives to virtue, decency, and morals in society." But who was to determine what particular acts were impeachable? Was the decision to rest on the caprice of ten or a hundred men in the community, or on federal or state statute and the provisions of the common law? Which if any of these laws had Chase violated? Whom had he offended? He had offended the House of Representatives. Was he to be impeached for that? Without using the phrase *ex post facto,* Hopkinson took up the theme:

"I maintain as a most important and indispensable principle, that no man should be criminally accused, no man can be criminally condemned, but for the violation of some known law by which he was bound to govern himself. Nothing is so necessary to justice and to safety as that the criminal code should be certain and known. Let the judge, as well as the citizen, precisely know the path he has to walk in, and what he may or may not do."

Can it be, asked Hopkinson, that the private citizen is protected "from the malice or caprice of any man or body of men, and can be brought into legal jeopardy only by the violation of laws before made known to him;" while the judge, on the contrary, "is to be exposed to punishment without knowing his offense, and the criminality or innocence of his conduct is to depend not upon the laws existing at the time, but upon the opinions of a body of men to be collected four or five years after the transaction?"

He answered:

"The Constitution, sir, never intended to lay the Judiciary thus prostrate at the feet of the House of Representatives, the slaves of their will, the victims of their caprice. The Judiciary must be protected from prejudice and varying opinions, or it is not worth a farthing."

Can the House of Representatives, asked Hopkinson, "create offenses at their will and pleasure, and declare that to be a crime in 1804 which was an indiscretion or pardonable error or perhaps an approved proceeding, in 1800? . . . If this be truly the case, if this power of impeachment may be thus extended without limit or control, then indeed is every valuable liberty prostrated at the foot of this omnipotent House of Representatives; and may God preserve us!"

Defense counsel Charles Lee contrasted Campbell's argument with the conflicting words of the Chase articles of impeachment. Campbell had denied the necessity of proving criminality; but Lee had been "led to believe that the present prosecution is brought before this honorable Court

as a court of criminal jurisdiction. . . . The articles themselves seem to have been drawn in conformity to this
opinion, for they all, except the fifth, charge, in express
terms, some criminal intention upon the respondent." It
was to be inferred from this "that a person is only impeachable for some criminal offense." He hardly needed to
ask what crime had been charged against Justice Chase;
none had been charged.

Defense council Luther Martin, like Hopkinson, took the
extreme stand that impeachment "must be for an indictable
offense." Quoting the clause on "high crimes and misdemeanors," he asked: "What is the true meaning of the word
'crime'? It is the breach of some law which renders the person who violates it liable to punishment. There can be no
crime committed where no such law is violated." What was
the meaning of "misdemeanor"? He quoted the new edition
of Jacob's *Law Dictionary:*

"Misdemesnor, or misdemeanor, a crime . . . [that] com-
prehends all indictable offenses which do not amount to
felony, as perjury, libels, conspiracies, assaults," etc.

He cited Blackstone's similar definition emphasizing its
further distinction between public and private wrongs, the
former constituting crimes and misdemeanors as offenses
against the whole community, while the latter "only entitle
the injured to a civil remedy."

As Hopkinson had done, Martin contended that the word
"high" applied to "misdemeanors" as well as to "crimes"
(an interpretation which House Manager Rodney freely
conceded), thus eliminating all indictable petty misdemeanors as grounds of impeachment. Martin declared:

"I am ready to go further and say, there may be instances
of very high crimes and misdemeanors, for which an officer
ought not to be impeached and removed from office; the
crimes ought to be such as to relate to his office, or which

tend to cover the person who committed them with turpitude and infamy; such as show there can be no dependance on that integrity and honor which will secure the performance of his official duties."

What would happen, Martin asked, if it were admitted that the House of Representatives has a right to impeach for acts which are not contrary to law, and that for such acts the Senate may convict and the officer may be removed? Admit that, he said, and "you leave your judges, and all your other officers, at the mercy of the prevailing party. You will place them much in the unhappy situation as were the people of England during the contest between the White and Red Roses, while the doctrine of constructive treasons prevailed. They must be the tools or the victims of the victorious party."

Under the Constitution, he declared, no judge or other officer can "be removed from office *but by impeachment,* and for the violation of *some law,* which violation must be not simply a crime or misdemeanor, but a *high* crime or misdemeanor." This principle, he said, had been contested that morning by a Manager (Caesar Rodney) who cited the constitution of the state of Pennsylvania, "by which he has told us a judge may, by the governor, be removed from office without the commission of any offense upon the vote of two-thirds of the two houses for his removal; notwithstanding that constitution has a similar provision for removal by impeachment as has the Constitution of the United States." Rodney had then inferred the existence of a similar power in the federal government. Martin said:

"To this I answer as we have no *such provision* in the Constitution of the United States the *reverse* is to be inferred, to wit, that the people of the United States from whom the Constitution emanated did not intend their judges should be removed, however obnoxious they might be to *any part* or to the *whole* of the Legislature, unless they were guilty of some high crime or misdemeanor, and then only by impeachment."

Having been a delegate to the Federal Convention, Martin could have stated his case more strongly. Possibly he had forgotten that this very power of "removal by address" was proposed on August 27, 1787, and that his own vote assisted in its overwhelming defeat. That record was still buried in secrecy at the time of Chase's trial.

Robert Goodloe Harper of the defense counsel then took up the theme of grounds for removal, driving hard at Manager Campbell's vulnerable position:

"Not content with endeavoring to blow up a flame of party spirit against the respondent . . . the honorable Managers have resorted to a principle as novel in our laws and jurisprudence, as it is subversive of the constitutional independence of the judicial department, and dangerous to the personal rights and safety of every man holding an office under this Government."

They have, said he, "contended 'that an impeachment is not a criminal prosecution, but an inquiry in the nature of an inquest of office, to ascertain whether a person holding an office be properly qualified for his situation; or whether it may not be expedient to remove him.' But if this principle be correct—if an impeachment be not indeed a criminal prosecution, but a mere inquest of office—if a conviction and removal on impeachment be indeed not a punishment, but the mere withdrawal of a favor of office granted—I ask why this formality of proceeding, this solemn apparatus of justice, this laborious investigation of facts?"

If the conviction of a judge on impeachment was not to

depend on his guilt or innocence of some crime alleged against him, continued Harper, "but on some reason of State policy or expediency, which may be thought by the House of Representatives, and two-thirds of the Senate, to require his removal, I ask why the solemn mockery of articles alleging high crimes and misdemeanors, of a court regularly formed, of a judicial oath administered to the members, of the public examination of witnesses, and of a trial conducted in all the usual forms? Why not settle this question of expediency, as all other questions of expediency are settled, by a reference to general political considerations, and in the usual mode of political discussion?"

Said Harper: "Everything by which we are surrounded informs us that we are in a court of law. Everything that we have been three weeks employed in doing reminds us that we are engaged not in a mere inquiry into the fitness of an officer for the place which he holds, but in the trial of a criminal case on legal principles." This he supported by quoting Wooddesson's lectures on the law of impeachment.

Harper then took up one by one the clauses of the Constitution pertaining to impeachment, to show their consistent employment of phrases relating to criminal law. With regard to the President's power to grant reprieves and pardons "for *offenses* against the United States except in cases of impeachment," was not this "the same thing as saying that cases of impeachment are cases of offenses"? Our law books "tell us that the word 'offense' means some violation of law. Whence it evidently follows that no officer of government can be impeached unless he has committed some violation of the law, either statute or common."

At this point Harper deviated from the position of his fellow counsel, and actually strengthened the Chase defense, by arguing that impeachable crimes and misdemean-

ors cannot be completely equated with indictable offenses.
"I can suppose cases where a judge ought to be impeached,"
he said, "for acts which I am not prepared to declare indictable. Suppose, for instance, that a judge should con-
stantly omit to hold court; or should habitually attend so
short a time each day as to render it impossible to despatch
the business." It might be open to question whether a judge
could be indicted for such sins of omission, though Harper
was inclined to think he could be:

"But I have no hesitation in saying that a judge in such
a case ought to be impeached. And this comes within the
principle for which I contend; for these acts of *culpable
omission* are a plain and direct violation of the law, which
commands him to hold courts a reasonable time for the
despatch of business; *and of his oath,* which binds him to
discharge faithfully and diligently the duties of his office."

Harper assailed the prosecution's heavy reliance on the
case of Judge Addison. That Pennsylvanian, Harper said,
was not removed, as the Managers contended, "for rude and
ungentlemanlike behavior in court to one of the colleagues,
but for a supposed usurpation of power." The charge was
that by an unlawful exertion of authority, he prevented
another sitting judge from exercising his lawful right to
charge a grand jury, and similar actions. If he did arbitrarily
prevent his colleague from exercising lawful rights, "he was
guilty of an offense for which he might properly be impeached; because he must in that case have acted in express
violation of the Constitution and laws." (Actually, as Governor McKean told Jefferson, Addison was removed because
he was an overactive Federalist.)

Harper then dealt with the argument of the Managers
that the clause on "high crimes and misdemeanors" was a
mere statement of what the punishment should be in spe-

cified cases, and that it did not debar impeachment for other causes. It must be remembered, he said, that the Constitution is a limited grant of power, and it is essential that such a grant be construed strictly, excluding all powers not conferred expressly or by necessary implication:

"When, therefore, the Constitution declares for what acts an officer shall be impeached, it gives power to impeach him for those acts and all power to impeach him for any other cause is withheld. The enumeration in the affirmative grant implies clearly a negative restriction, as to all cases not enumerated. This provision of the Constitution, therefore, must be considered, upon every sound principle of construction, as a declaration that no impeachment shall lie except for a crime or misdemeanor; in other words, for a criminal violation of some law."

Continuing his recital of the vocabulary of crime in the constitutional clauses on impeachment, Harper took up the phrase "impeachment for and *conviction* of" treason, etc. This term "conviction," he said, "has in our law a fixed and appropriate meaning. . . . It always imports the decision of a competent tribunal, pronouncing a person guilty of some specific offense, for which he has been legally brought to trial."

Harper next took up one by one the impeachment laws of Pennsylvania, Delaware, Maryland, Virginia, the two Carolinas, and Vermont, showing that they universally made judges impeachable for "crimes and offenses," "misdemeanors," "misbehavior in office" (having the same legal meaning, he said, as "misdemeanor"), and "corruption"— all connoting criminality. In Vermont the power was "to impeach State criminals."

"Need I," asked Harper, "urge the necessity of adhering to those principles as it respects the independence of the judiciary department? Need I enlarge on the essential importance of that independence to the security of personal rights, and to the well being, nay, to the existence of a free government?"

Observance of settled constitutional principles in cases of impeachment was important not only "to the party accused, to posterity, and to the interests of free Governments." It was equally so to the character and feelings of all the men upon the bench. "Were causes like this to be determined on expediency, and not on fixed principles of law, to what suspicions might not the judges be liable, of subordinating the public good to selfish ends?" Harper concluded:

"In every light, therefore, in which this great principle can be viewed, whether as a well-established doctrine of the Constitution; as the bulwark of personal safety and judicial independence . . . it will, I trust, be established so as never hereafter to be brought into question, that an impeachment is not a mere inquiry, in the nature of an inquest of office, whether an officer be qualified for his place, or whether some reason of policy or expediency may not demand his removal, but a criminal prosecution for the support of which the proof of a willful violation of a known law of the land is known to be indispensably required."

Harper's speech, so different from his conduct as a House Manager in the Blount trial, left the case against Justice Chase in a shambles. He had demolished Campbell's "inquest of office" concept of impeachment, and at the same time, by substituting "some known law" for "indictable offense," he had rescued his own side from the too narrow restriction proposed by Hopkinson and Martin. The Managers were left with no apparent recourse, on the basis of their past presentation, except to prove the unprovable: that Justice Chase had engaged in noncriminal activities made impeachable by impure and corrupt motives.

Manager Joseph H. Nicholson then undertook to salvage the situation by repudiating his colleague Campbell (even denying he heard what is on the record) and launching an entirely new line of argument. He said:

"We were also told by the honorable counsel for the accused that when we found the accusation shrunk from the testimony, and that the case could no longer be supported, we resorted to the forlorn hope of contending that an impeachment was not a criminal prosecution, but a mere inquest of office. For myself, I am free to declare, that I heard no such position taken. If declarations of this kind have been made, in the name of the Managers, I here disclaim them. We do contend that this is a criminal prosecution, for offenses committed in the discharge of high official duties, and we now support it, not merely for the purpose of removing an individual from office, but in order that the punishment inflicted on him may deter others from pursuing the baneful example which has been set them."

Then, to combat the argument of Hopkinson and Martin that "no judge can be impeached and removed from office for any act or offense for which he could not be indicted," Nicholson took an entirely new line. There was no need to prove indictable "crimes and misdemeanors," he averred, because impeachment could be grounded on absence of "good behavior":

"The Constitution declares that 'the judges both of the supreme and inferior courts shall hold their commissions during good behavior.' The plain and correct inference to be drawn from this language is that a judge is to hold his office so long as he demeans himself well in it; and when-

ever he shall not demean himself well, he shall be removed.
I therefore contend that a judge would be liable to impeachment under the Constitution even without the insertion of
that clause [about high crimes and misdemeanors]. . . . The
nature of the tenure by which a judge holds his office is
such that for any act of misbehavior in office he is liable
to removal."

This opinion, put forth in desperation, was weighted
with the sanctity of antiquity. Nicholson traced the phrase
"during good behavior" back to a statute of Henry VIII,
where it came into the law in its Latin form *durante se
bene gesserit*. The statute provided for the appointment of
a county *custos rotulorum* (keeper of the rolls) and a clerk
of the peace, the former to be removable at will, the latter
to "hold his office *durante se bene gesserit*." The statute
declared, said Nicholson, that "ignorant and unlearned
persons" had wormed their way into those offices:

"The reason for making the tenure to be during good
behavior was that the office had been held by incapable
persons, who were too ignorant to discharge the duties;
and it was certainly the intention of the legislature that
such persons would be removed whenever their incapacity
was discovered. Under this statute, therefore, I think it
clear that the officer holding his office during good behavior
might be removed for any improper exercise of his powers,
whether arising from ignorance, corruption, passion or any
other cause."

Nicholson's exposition of that law, enacted in 1535, was
thoroughly misleading. The statute (37 Henry 8.) had
nothing to do with the removal of judges or with impeachment. Yet it has often been cited without investigation—
most recently in the proceedings against Justice Douglas—
as a conclusive British precedent for *removal of judges by
impeachment* without finding them guilty of any high

crime or misdemeanor. Here is its true history and nature:

Before its enactment, the statute says, both the *custos* and the clerk of the peace, whom the *custos* appointed, had tenure for life, "whereby great misdemeanors had been." Accordingly, the *custos* was made removable by the Crown. The *custos* retained authority to "appoint the clerk of the peace who is to hold office so long as the other should continue *custos,* so as he demean himself well in the office." Thus the clerk, who had clerical and magisterial duties under the justices of the peace, was made *removable for cause, by the keeper of the rolls* who appointed him.

It is nonsense to equate such a statute with the impeachment of justices of the United States Supreme Court for "high crimes and misdemeanors." Yet the misrepresentation goes further still. In 1689, following the "Glorious Revolution," the 1535 statute was revised to strike out the words "so long as the other should continue *custos.*" That change produced life tenure for the clerk, instead of tenure during the tenure of the *custos,* subject to good behavior. The next clause provided that "if any clerk of the peace do misdemean himself in the office, upon complaint in writing to the justices at the quarter session they may remove or suspend him." Pointing to the principal evil, the law commanded that the clerk, before taking office, make oath that he did not and would not pay "any money or reward . . . for such nomination or appointment."

This law of 1689 had another effect. It brought the clerk of the peace within the compass of a 1552 statute of Edward VI providing a method of removal by judges. As described in *Comyn's Digest of the Laws of England,* the 1552 statute covered all officers "which concern the administration or execution of justice . . . in the spiritual court . . . as well as officers in the courts of common law. . . . And, regularly, there must be a *scire facias* to remove the party, where he has the office as a matter of record; for he cannot be removed without matter of record."

Where does this leave the congressional definers of tenure "during good behavior"? If British statutes on removal of clerks to British justices of the peace are incorporated by implication in the Constitution of the United States, the process by which these clerks are removed must be equally binding. And since in England it is a process separate from impeachment, it must likewise be separate here.

The result would be a situation in which any federal district judge, on receiving a complaint in writing, could summon the Chief Justice of the United States on a writ of *scire facias* and order him out of office. Yet that is no more fantastic than the illustration actually given by Nicholson to support his system of removal by impeachment for want of "good behavior." He said:

"There are offenses for which an officer may be impeached, and against which there are no known positive laws. It is possible that the day may arrive when a President of the United States, having some great political object in view, may endeavor to influence the Legislature by holding out threats or inducements to them. . . . The hope of office may be held out to a Senator; and I think it cannot be doubted, that for this the President would be liable to impeachment, although there is no positive law forbidding it."

If Congress pursued that concept of constitutional law with sufficient zeal and attention to evidence, there would be a long line of Presidential gravestones in Arlington National Cemetery, each bearing the inscription *Removed from Office by Impeachment*. Incredible as it seems, this and lesser grounds are within the compass of the impeaching power as it was stated by Minority Leader Ford on April 15, 1970: "The only honest answer is that an impeachable offense is whatever a majority of the House of Representatives considers it to be at a given moment in history."

In the Chase trial, Manager Caesar Rodney pursued Nicholson's theme of general power to remove a judge for a lapse from "good behavior" without having committed any crime. Rodney clung to the position that the clause providing for removal of the President, Vice President, and all other civil officers for "treason, bribery or other high crimes and misdemeanors" does not determine who may be impeached, and for what offenses. With consummate assurance he declared that this clause, "in plain English," commands "upon the conviction by impeachment of *certain* atrocious offenses that the guilty officer shall be removed *at all events.*" The framers, he said, feared that "awed by fear or seduced by favor, the constitutional judges would not hurl him at once from the seat which he was unworthy to occupy."

But, continued Rodney, "I submit with due deference . . . that there are other cases than those here specified for which an impeachment will lay and is the proper remedy." That power was contained in the clause specifying that judges "shall hold their offices during good behavior. . . . If a judge misbehaved he ought to be removed, because agreeably to the plainest provision he has forfeited his right to hold the office." When a judge (meaning Chase) was guilty of "behavior, the most rude and contumelious . . . truly degrading on the bench and unquestionably criminal," was he to remain on the bench because "no indictment would lay for the same"? He cited half a dozen perverse actions a judge might take or omit—acts of favoritism or prejudice, systematic buffoonery on the bench, dereliction of duty—all in violation of his oath of office. Could he not be impeached for such conduct?

Rodney's argument was pointless. Of course a judge could be impeached if he willfully violated his oath of office; and such knowing misconduct was within the scope of defense counsel Harper's impeachable "violation of known law." The oath of office is a positive law; *deliberate* violation of it is "high misdemeanor." Rodney was forced to misrepresent the defense's position in order to bolster the product of his and Nicholson's imagination: the supposition that the words "during good behavior" imply a sweeping, indefinite extension of impeachable offenses beyond the high crimes and misdemeanors laid down in the Constitution.

If we assume that Nicholson and Rodney were sincere in their belief that tenure "during good behavior" implies an unwritten extension of the specified grounds of impeachment, they can be forgiven the error because the *Debates* of the Federal Convention—which prove them wrong— were not published until 1840. But what can be said for those who in 1970, after reading the framers' words to the contrary, cited Nicholson and Rodney as valid authorities because they spoke so soon after the drafting of the Constitution?

John Randolph, chairman of the House Managers, closed the Chase trial for the prosecution. He began by assailing the original Hopkinson argument that a civil officer could be impeached only for an indictable offense, and ended by accepting Harper's extension to include offenses "committed against some known law." "Well," said Randolph, "take the question in this point of view, and there is no longer matter of dispute between us. . . . For what do we contend?—that the respondent has contravened the known law of the land"—his oath of office—which required him "to dispense justice faithfully and impartially, and without respect to persons." Said Randolph:

"He stands charged with having sinned against this law

and against his sacred oath, by acting in his judicial capacity unfaithfully, partially, and with respect to persons. These are our points. We DO charge him with misdemeanor in office. We aver that he hath demeaned himself amiss— partially, unfaithfully, unjustly, corruptly."

Thus Randolph, alone among the House Managers, presented grounds of impeachment that were in accord with the Constitution, both in its wording and in the revelations of intent discovered later in the debates of the constitutional convention. But his charges against Justice Chase fell apart on two words quoted above, "unfaithfully" and "corruptly."

Chase was a bad judge, though one of great learning. His conduct was unfair, partial, biased, and oppressive; but everything he did was done in the belief that he was serving his country nobly, saving it from enemies foreign and domestic: from France, from Jefferson, and from the whole Democratic opposition that swelled into a majority because of the foreign policy madness and domestic insanity of the Adams administration. The Constitution did not make honest error impeachable, and Chase incontestably was both honest and in error.

The Senate so found. With six and sometimes more Jeffersonians joining the Federalists, the Senate on March 1, 1805, acquitted Justice Chase on every count. One vote was unanimous. The nearest approach to conviction came on the final article charging delivery of "an intemperate and inflammatory political harangue" to a Maryland grand jury. Here the vote was guilty, 18; not guilty, 16. By that division the ruling party refused to exercise its numerical power to remove a judge from political motives, in defiance of the Constitution.

By the united force of this bipartisan phalanx, the Senate's verdict struck a mighty blow against the grafting of British impeachment excesses onto the carefully restricted clauses of the United States Constitution. It appeared to be settled law that justices of the Supreme Court could be removed from office only for "high crimes and misdemeanors" which were either serious indictable offenses or willful violations of their oath of office. These were the constitutional criteria by which departure from "good behavior" was to be measured.

Was this decision unchangeable? No, two thirds of the Senate could overset it in any subsequent impeachment trial. Yet so great was the impact of the Chase acquittal that a hundred years elapsed before the sophistries of Nicholson and Rodney again emerged in congressional impeachment proceedings. One hundred and sixty-five years went by before they were surpassed in unconstitutionality by legislators attempting to impeach Douglas. In both attempts the motive was the same—to remake the Supreme Court for partisan purposes.

CHAPTER V

JUSTICE DOUGLAS
AND JOHN MARSHALL

CHIEF JUSTICE JOHN MARSHALL sighed with relief when the Senate acquitted Associate Justice Chase. Ever since President Jefferson had induced Congress to repeal the 1801 law creating the "midnight judges," and especially while the case of *Marbury* v. *Madison* was pending in the Supreme Court, rumors of impeachments had been in the air. Belief was almost universal that the Supreme Court would order delivery of the withheld judicial commissions and that the Jefferson administration would strike back at the Court. Marshall's biographer Alfred J. Beveridge may have exaggerated the actual danger, but he clearly reflected the apprehension of the Chief Justice when he wrote:

"There was a particular and powerful reason for Marshall to fear impeachment and removal from office; for, should he be deposed, it was certain that Jefferson would appoint Spencer Roane of Virginia to be Chief Justice of the United States . . . [and] the Supreme Court would become an

(84)

engine for the destruction of every theory of government which Marshall held dear."

Six weeks after the House of Representatives impeached Justice Chase, the newly elected Senator John Quincy Adams recorded in his diary the reason why, as given by his colleague William B. Giles of Virginia: "We want your offices, for the purpose of giving them to men who will fill them better." In the same fireside conversation, Giles turned to a wavering senator of his own party (Israel Smith of Vermont) and said, concerning the recent decision in *Marbury* v. *Madison:*

"If the Judges of the Supreme Court should dare, as they had done, to declare acts of Congress unconstitutional . . . it was the undoubted right of the House to impeach them, and of the Senate to remove them for giving such opinions, however honest or sincere they may have been in entertaining them."

Not only should Chase be removed by impeachment, Giles declared, but so should all other members "except the last one appointed" (Justice William Johnson, a Jefferson choice). The purpose was clear, wrote Adams: to sweep "the supreme judicial bench clean at a stroke."

The menace of impeachment hanging over Marshall's head goes far to explain the peculiar nature of the 1803 *Marbury* decision, in which the great permanent objective of the Chief Justice—to establish the power of the Supreme Court to hold acts of Congress unconstitutional—was employed for his own protection. He used it to deny the Court's power, conferred by Congress in its statute of 1789, to issue writs of mandamus; therefore the Court could not compel the Secretary of State to deliver commissions to the "midnight judges" appointed by President Adams. Thus, if the remarks of Senator Giles represented Presidential intentions rather than his own extremism, the program was set back by Marshall's *Marbury* strategy and utterly destroyed by the Chase acquittal. Incredible as it seems, Senator Giles, either won over by defense counsel or vexed with the President, was one of the six Republicans who saved Chase from removal and thus preserved the independence of the judiciary.

Had Justice Chase been removed on grounds that so clearly violated the Constitution, in a trial instigated by partisan politics, it would not inevitably have led to a succession of such prosecutions. No other member of the Court was as vulnerable to the charge of biased conduct. Nevertheless, the menace of removal would have hung over the whole Marshall Court, impeding freedom of thought and action during its highly controversial existence. Mighty passions were stirred by the repeated confrontations of state and federal sovereignty and the steady succession of decisions upholding national supremacy. Newspapers were filled with denunciatory articles written by public men, including jurists, and signed with pseudonyms. The Chief Justice himself published eleven unsigned articles, whose authorship was an open secret, defending his decision in *McCulloch* v. *Maryland* against the strictures of Spencer Roane, Virginia's foremost jurist. And Marshall furnished abundant openings for personal attacks of the sort leveled against Justice Douglas.

There are in fact striking parallels between the actual impeachment of Justice Chase, the charges made against Justice Douglas, and the hypothetical grounds of impeachment of Chief Justice Marshall—all in violation of constitutional restrictions. The most impressive resemblance involves the spirit though not the letter of the Constitution— the actual political pressure for impeachment of Chase and Douglas, and the theoretical openings for such an unwarranted move against Marshall. To present the three cases in cameo:

Chase was impeached for political reasons, on a true set of facts which did not meet the constitutional requirements for impeachment.

Douglas was accused in a set of charges which, as investigated and dismissed by the special subcommittee of the Judiciary Committee, consisted of (1) charges that were impeachable but false, (2) those that were both false and nonimpeachable, and (3) those that were true but were neither impeachable nor discreditable.

Marshall laid himself wide open to accusations similar to those made against Justice Douglas, none of them impeachable under a proper interpretation of the Constitution.

Initiation of the moves against Chase and Douglas involved what might be called "similarity by contrast." Both cases grew out of their official actions as judges. In that capacity Justice Chase, holding circuit court, repeatedly denied American citizens their civil rights and liberties; he was a conspicuous champion of political repression, represented by the Sedition Act of 1798. Justice Douglas, during thirty-one years on the Court, had been the most outspoken member, first of a growing minority, then of a majority, that rescued the Bill of Rights from a century of neglect and suppression.

The conduct of Justice Chase aroused the active hostility of the political party, headed by Thomas Jefferson, that struggled with and finally triumphed over the semimonarchic forces of entrenched wealth and privilege. The conduct of Justice Douglas aroused equal hostility among the spiritual descendants of the Americans who imposed the Sedition Act upon the country.

However, the methods by which the impeachment process was invoked in the two cases were very different. The Chase impeachment was initiated through pressure by President Jefferson—pressure unacknowledged but known to the entire country—based on actions variously construed but substantially undenied. The Douglas impeachment attempt had its origin in a union of three groups in the House of Representatives with distinct but overlapping motives: (1) Southern segregationists, with Representative Joe Waggonner of Louisiana as their spokesman, (2) Northern anti-libertarians, headed by Representative Louis C. Wyman of New Hampshire—who as state attorney general outdid all other witch-hunters in the country except for Senator Joe McCarthy, and (3) Republican Minority Leader Gerald C. Ford of Michigan, pushing President Nixon's project of building a Supreme Court that would undo the libertarian innovations of the Warren Court. The most potent force was the anger of President Nixon and of Southern congressmen over the Senate's rejection of two Presidential nominees to the Supreme Court, Clement Haynsworth of South Carolina and G. Harrold Carswell of Florida.

Douglas was a natural target for these groups because of both his outspoken liberalism and his extensive extrajudicial activities. His vulnerability is well summed up in the report of the special subcommittee of the House Committee on the Judiciary, which investigated all charges and cleared him:

"Throughout his career in the Government, and during his service as Associate Justice, William O. Douglas has asserted strong convictions on a variety of subjects. . . . He has expressed the 'strict constructionist' view of the First Amendment that Congress lacks power to enact laws to restrict speech, press or peaceable assembly.* He has been

---

* The words "strict constructionist" should be read carefully by those, including President Nixon, who regard strict construction of the First Amendment as "loose construction."

outspoken on his concepts of unreasonable search and seizure, the privilege against self-incrimination, the right to
counsel and technological intrusion on the right to privacy.
He has joined in judicial rulings in these fields that have
dismayed some advocates of 'strict' law enforcement for
crime prevention and has been an outstanding, energetic
advocate of natural resource conservation, and wilderness
preservation. In short, in these and other fields, Associate
Justice Douglas has taken an activist role and established
intellectual positions in controversial matters that clearly
are not shared by all, or perhaps in some instances, by even
many of his fellow citizens."

Aggravating the situation, but properly ignored by the
subcommittee, was the widespread popular resentment
against Douglas's three divorces and fourth marriage. With
some this was a genuine grievance; with others, a political
weapon.

Douglas, the report goes on to say, "is noted for his
tremendous energy. He has long been recognized as one of
the workhorses of the Court. His extra judicial activities
have not diminished the volume of his work for the Court."
During twenty-three of his thirty-one years on the Court,
the Committee found, he ranked either first or second in
number of opinions written; and this was true in six out of
his last ten years. Justice Tom C. Clark, shortly before he
resigned from the Court, gave the author of this book an
explanation of his colleague's extraordinary output of legal
opinions, books, articles and lectures. "Bill Douglas," he
said, "possesses a chain-lightning mind," enabling him to
think and write much faster than any of his colleagues.

The principal demand for impeachment of Justice Douglas was made by Representative Ford on April 15, 1970, in
a long speech replete with polemical invective. In its course
he was interrupted by Representative Andrew Jacobs, Jr.,

of Indiana, friendly to Douglas, who challenged the Republican leader to introduce a resolution directly impeaching the justice. Mr. Ford refused to do so. Thereupon Jacobs himself introduced an impeachment resolution, and it was adopted by the House.

Why this strategy? Because the Ford-Wyman-Waggonner plan was to move the creation of a special committee of the House to inquire into the charges. Any motion to create a special committee would be referred automatically to the House Rules Committee, chaired by a Mississippi segregationist. A direct motion for impeachment would be referred automatically to the House Committee on the Judiciary, chaired by Congressman Emanuel Celler of New York. So, instead of a possible Roman saturnalia of public accusation and innuendo as the Rules Committee determined whether an impeachment resolution should be presented, the actual impeachment motion could be expected to produce a thorough and impartial inquiry into all the allegations made by Douglas's accusers.

The special subcommittee, appointed by Chairman Celler, consisted of himself, Byron G. Rogers of Colorado, and Jack Brooks of Texas, Democrats; Edward Hutchinson of Michigan and William E. McCulloch of Ohio, Republicans. They devoted five months to the work and issued a final report of 924 pages completely clearing Justice Douglas of all charges. The report falls into two parts: 7 pages devoted to concepts of impeachment, and 917 pages to the guilt or innocence of Justice Douglas. The brief section on concepts, totally ignored in press reports, is the more important: it represents, for the first time in more than a century and a half, a return to the principles that prevailed in the acquittal of Justice Chase. The subcommittee's final recommendations read in full:

1. "It is not necessary for the members of the Judiciary

Committee to take a position on either of the concepts of impeachment discussed in Chapter II.

2. "Intensive investigation of the Special Subcommittee has not disclosed creditable evidence that would warrant preparation of charges on any acceptable concept of an impeachable offense."

Celler, Rogers, and Brooks signed the report. McCulloch neither signed nor dissented. Hutchinson dissented, objecting principally to the presentation of concepts of impeachment that were not necessary to a decision, and saying that he was not satisfied on two points regarding Justice Douglas's conduct. These points were so trivial that, like the silence of Representative McCulloch, his dissent indicated Republican unwillingness to clash with Minority Leader Ford.

The importance of the campaign against Justice Douglas lies not in its outcome (it was doomed to failure from the start) but in its climactic place in the growth of congressional pretensions to power not conferred by the Constitution. The attempt stands out in menacing contrast to the restriction of that power in the Chase impeachment and the absence of any such move in Congress against the most controversial figure in Supreme Court history—Chief Justice John Marshall.

After the appointment of the special subcommittee, Douglas placed all his files at its disposal and retained Judge Simon H. Rifkind of New York City as his attorney. The Jacobs resolution specified no offenses, but the special subcommittee took cognizance of all the charges made in Ford's speech, the accusations contained in resolutions moved by Congressman Wyman and others, and all material received from government agencies. Thus, unofficially, Ford became House Manager of impeachment proceedings. In that capacity he retained Detroit lawyer Bethel B. Kelley as his legal adviser. Both Rifkind and Kelley presented written briefs and rebuttals. These, together with Ford's April 15 speech, the Wyman resolutions, and a speech by Representative Paul N. McCloskey, Jr., of California defending Douglas, were published in one or another of the special subcommittee's three reports.

The charges against Douglas centered on his connection with the philanthropic Albert Parvin Foundation in Los Angeles, of which he served as president at a salary of $12,000 a year from January 1, 1961, until he resigned in May 1969. There was nothing illegal in his holding the post, but the objection was raised that a member of the Supreme Court ought not to have any financial connection with an outside institution. This phase of the "impeachment" cry was abruptly dropped in 1969, when Senate hearings disclosed that Circuit Judge Warren Burger, nominated for Chief Justice, had received $7,500 as a consultant to the Mayo Foundation of Minnesota. Later, both the accusers and defenders of Douglas joined in unanimous confirmation to the Supreme Court of United States District Judge Harry Blackmun, a former tax lawyer, after he revealed that during his tenure on the bench he had received $8,500 as coexecutor of several estates. In harmony with the Senate's unanimous actions, the special subcommittee absolved both Burger and Blackmun, along with Douglas, in its comments on the latter's general connection with the Albert Parvin Foundation:

"At the time these discussions were held and the arrangements entered into there was no suggestion that a judge or a justice could not provide service to a charitable foundation and receive compensation therefor. No law is violated, and the Canons of Judicial Ethics permit comparable activities. The only restraint is that the charitable

service not interfere with the discharge of judicial responsibilities."

Absolution on this count left standing a more substantial
accusation against Justice Douglas: that in the process of
organizing the Albert Parvin Foundation he had drafted
the articles of incorporation. If that was true it furnished
technical, though paltry, grounds of impeachment for violation of an act of Congress prohibiting the practice of law
by federal judges. That would be a "high misdemeanor."
The special subcommittee investigated the charge and
found conclusive documentary proof that it was untrue.

A third charge related to the endowment of the foundation. Albert Parvin is a multimillionaire Los Angeles manu-
facturer of hotel and motel equipment. The Flamingo
Hotel Company of Las Vegas, Nevada, bought its furnish-
ings from the Albert Parvin Company and defaulted on its
payments. Parvin bought the hotel, which, like others in
Las Vegas, operated a gambling casino under state license.
He held the Flamingo for two years and sold it at a profit
of $2,500,000. The Flamingo Company was liquidated, and
the promissory notes of the new hotel owners were placed
in a custodial account in the Bank of America for collec-
tion.

It was soon after this that Justice Douglas and Parvin
became acquainted, at a Douglas lecture in Santa Barbara.
The popular conception of their relationship, drawn from
newspaper stories and congressional speeches, is that Douglas, enticed by $12,000 a year, consented to have his name
used by Albert Parvin to give prestige to his private foundation, regardless of its purposes. The special subcommittee
found its very different origin described in the following
letter from Parvin to Douglas, written July 25, 1960:

"Recently a friend of mine gave me a copy of *America*

Challenged [a book by Douglas]. So moved and impressed was I by its contents, that it gave spark to an idea that has emboldened me for many years. It is regrettable that with the billions spent for ways to destroy civilization, so little is available to promote better understanding amongst nations and their peoples through education; so well pointed out in your book.

"It is my desire to endow a trust or foundation for the sole purpose of promulgating and promoting better relations amongst nations through education. Perhaps the slogan could be 'Survival through Education' since peace in our time seems unattainable. One of its functions would be that of awarding a prize or prizes, annually, to the individual or group that has made the greatest contribution toward that accomplishment.

"Being a layman of limited capacities in such undertakings, I, therefore, seek your aid and advice. . . . I would be highly honored if you would aid in establishing and directing the functional and administrative policies of this foundation. It is my intention to reimburse you for all expenses involved and in addition thereto pay you an annual fee or salary for your services in connection therewith."

To establish this foundation, Parvin said, he had "some 2 to 2½ million dollars" in stocks and interest-bearing notes. Douglas replied that he would be happy to serve as a trustee and an officer. The Flamingo promissory notes, as they were collected by the Bank of America, gave the Foundation a $2,000,000 endowment. This was enlarged between 1961 and 1965 by gifts of 31,000 shares of the stock of the Parvin-Dohrmann Corporation, a company listed on the American Stock Exchange, formed through the Parvin Company's acquisition of a company manufacturing kitchen equipment.

From the Parvin and Douglas files the special subcommittee found that Justice Douglas refused a salary of $20,000, preferring to serve without compensation. He then was voted a salary of $12,000 plus expenses, but he refused to collect expenses and said that he would treat the salary (after income tax) as an expense account. His expenses included numerous trips from Washington to Los Angeles and to foreign countries.

The Albert Parvin Foundation devoted almost its entire annual income to supporting and supervising Parvin Fellowships at Princeton University and the University of California in Los Angeles. Men between the ages of twenty-five and thirty-five who were regarded as potential leaders were brought to these schools from Asia, Africa, and Latin America. Douglas said in a letter to Chief Justice Warren on October 31, 1966:

"We chose men in government, in journalism, in education, our hope being that after exposure to both the theory and the practical operations of a free society, they would return to their countries with new insight into how the forces of communism could be combated. We have been very proud of their achievements. Many of them have already moved into important positions in their native countries, and we are confident that over the years we will produce many Prime Ministers, many Secretaries of State, many journalists, many professors, all dedicated to the democratic cause."

What most angered Gerald Ford and Louis Wyman was Douglas's and the Parvin Foundation's connection with the Center for the Study of Democratic Institutions at Santa Barbara. In his speech of April 15, 1970, Ford inveighed against this tax-exempt organization whose operations, he said, were responsible for "the birth of the New Left as a political movement." He declared that Wyman had investigated the institution, run by "Dr. Robert Hutchins and his intellectual incubators for the New Left and the SDS, and others of the same ilk," and had "discovered that the Associate Justice has been receiving money from it."

To be sure he had: $500 per lecture, of which he gave several each year. It was the same honorarium paid to numerous members of Congress, other public officials, educators, clergymen, and editors. Judge Rifkind's "Douglas Fact Brief" named some of the participants in Center programs: Chief Justice Warren Burger when he was on the circuit bench; Associate Justice Byron White when he was in the Justice Department; Senators John Sherman Cooper of Kentucky and Jennings Randolph of West Virginia; Charles Yost, ambassador to the United Nations; Derek Bok, now president of Harvard University; Paul Freund of the Harvard Law School; William Buckley, right-wing editor and columnist. The Center sought expression of all points of view; its aim was to be a catalyst of public opinion, and Justice Douglas promoted that purpose, both as a paid participant in the programs and as an unpaid director of the institution.

Further outraging the conservatives in Congress was Douglas's short book, *Points of Rebellion,* which sought to explain the current unrest of young people and to point a way through it. Gerald Ford characterized the book as "a fuzzy harangue evidently intended to give historic legitimacy to the militant hippie-yippie movement and to bear testimony that a 71-year-old Justice of the Supreme Court is one in spirit with them." Ford conceded that the First Amendment protected the right of Justice Douglas "to write and print this drivel." But, he said, "I wonder if it can be deemed 'good behavior' in the constitutional sense for such a distorted diatribe against the Government of the United States to be published, indeed publicly autographed [his signature was printed on the cover] and promoted, by an Associate Justice of the Supreme Court."

Congressman Wyman echoed this line of argument in his House Resolution 922, which did not come to a vote. However, the special subcommittee gave full consideration to these denunciations. It was not clear, said its report, whether publication of any book could afford the basis of impeachment. As for this one:

"Analysis by the Special Subcommittee indicates that Justice Douglas' critics have misinterpreted the meaning of the book. *Points of Rebellion* does not call for violent overthrow of established order in this country. It does not sanction rebellion. The book is not a neutral document; it has a clearly defined thesis. Far from advocating violence, the book urges a reordering of priorities through the traditional legal channels to avoid the violence which the author believes is inevitable if the established order does not accommodate to the needs of disillusioned segments of the society."

The special subcommittee reproduced Wyman's quotations from *Points of Rebellion* as he had presented them, out of context and out of order. It then reproduced the same quotations in their true order and context, whereupon the implication of every passage quoted by Wyman was reversed.*

---

* To fully realize the effectiveness of the Wyman system, consider the following imaginary conversation between a college radical and a heckler, first as spoken, then as it might be quoted to promote repressive legislation:

Heckler: "What would you think about the assassination of the President?"

College Radical: "I should think it might be considered a good idea by somebody intent on plunging the country into a boiling cauldron of repression."

As edited for publication:

A closely related ground of impeachment was that Douglas sold reproduction rights for one chapter of *Points of Rebellion* to a pornographic magazine, the *Evergreen Review*. From the testimony of Douglas and the publisher, and from the correspondence that passed between them immediately after the sale, the special subcommittee found that the publisher, Random House, had made the sale "without Justice Douglas' consent and without his knowledge." Hundreds of authors can testify that this is not an uncommon practice.

Douglas's "high misdemeanor" in taking the liberal side is illumined by another paragraph in the Wyman impeachment resolution charging that the justice, "contrary to his sworn obligation to refrain therefrom . . . repeatedly engaged in political activity while an incumbent of the High Court." The illustrations given were his "continued public advocacy of the recognition of Red China by the United States" and his effort to bring about a "detente with the Soviet Union." If political activity while on the Court, as such, constitutes grounds of impeachment, Douglas would be equally impeachable if he continually opposed recognition of Red China or if he argued against an understanding with Russia.

There has been nothing comparable to such grounds of criticism since 1812, when the American declaration of war on England convinced the Federalist Party that President James Madison was making the United States the junior partner of Napoleon Bonaparte. Who could save the coun-

---

Heckler: "What would you think about the assassination of the President?"

College Radical: "I should think it might be considered a good idea."

By similar editing Congressman Wyman, quoting from *Points of Rebellion,* made it appear that Justice Douglas equated the conduct of the American government with the tactics of Adolf Hitler.

try from the disaster of Madison's reelection? Nobody but a Virginian, and no Virginian except John Marshall. The Chief Justice, personally friendly to Madison but bitterly opposed to the war, shied away from the political overtures but endorsed the objective. To defeat Madison, he wrote to the President's ousted Secretary of State, Robert Smith:

"All minor considerations should be waived; the lines of subdivision between parties, if not absolutely effaced, should at least be convened for a time; and the great division between the friends of peace and the advocates of war ought alone to remain."

One can imagine the tumult if a letter with similar wording should come to light today, written by Justice Douglas to the Nixon-purged New York Senator Charles Goodell, on the best strategy for preventing Nixon's reelection because of his conduct of the war in Indo-China.

Must a member of the Supreme Court refrain from any expression of controversial views, thus becoming a political eunuch? Or must he merely avoid any political activity that affronts the conservative part of the community? Suppose that Justice Douglas, or Chief Justice Marshall, participated in an outside activity which was not only explosively controversial, but threatened to impinge upon his work as a member of the Court. To take an extreme case, suppose Douglas should accept a position as president or vice president of the National Association for the Advancement of Colored People. Would that furnish constitutional grounds of impeachment? No, but it would be the gravest sort of impropriety, and might sweep him off the bench.

In the early nineteenth century the American Colonization Society was the nearest counterpart to the NAACP. Organized in 1816 for the purpose of resettling American blacks in a section of Africa that was given the name of Liberia, its first activity was to finance passage for free

Negroes and to help them establish themselves there. In the background, however, was the hope of eliminating slavery by this method. For a time many prominent slaveholders shared the hope, but it gradually faded as the cotton gin tied the South more closely to slave labor and bound slavery more tightly upon the South. By 1830 the American Colonization Society was engaged in a full-scale campaign of purchase, manumission, and resettlement of slaves. It began to call for use of federal and state funds for the palpable but undeclared purpose of wiping out the whole institution of slavery. Southern slaveholders reacted ever more violently against the ACS program as a threat to the social order— and to their economic existence.

What would have been said if a justice of the Supreme Court had been elected president or vice president of the American Colonization Society? Yet one was elected, and he accepted the office: in January 1832, Chief Justice Marshall became one of the society's twenty-four vice presidents.

Marshall's work against slavery had begun earlier. In 1829 he and James Madison took the lead in organizing the Colonization Society of Virginia. In 1831 Marshall was elected president of the state society, Madison vice president. Scorning the pretense (which still prevailed in Maryland) that the object was merely to transport free blacks, Marshall and Madison asked the Virginia legislature in January 1832 to aid the movement with public funds. As members of the society, their petition read, they would express no views on slavery, but "as citizens and lovers of Virginia, we await in common with our whole community . . . relief from an oppressive evil."

The Virginia legislature, thoroughly in the grip of the slavery forces, rejected the appeal. The petition was published at just about the time Marshall became a vice president of the national society. Two months later (March 28, 1832) Senator Robert Y. Hayne of South Carolina, a leading defender of slavery, launched a violent attack upon the society. He denounced its effort to finance a joint public and private colonization program by means of the sale of public lands—a program which, if written into law, was sure to be carried to the Supreme Court on the hotly controversial issue of the power of Congress to appropriate for the general welfare. Hayne struck both at that power and at the program's transparent purpose of doing away with slavery, saying:

"He must be blind who did not see that, if the powers of the General Government were conceded to carry into effect the first preliminary measures of the Society, the colonization of the free people of color, its power to accomplish the ultimate object in view, the removal of the whole of the African race from the United States, would, in due time, be claimed as a necessary consequence. . . . [W]henever the General Government should assert the power to levy and appropriate money, or to apply the public lands toward the objects of the Colonization Society, it would immediately lead to the consequences which he had deprecated."

Although the American Colonization Society was not functionally engaged in litigation, as is the NAACP, Senator Hayne's speech made it clear that there would be an epochal contest in the Supreme Court if such an appropriation were made. It also revealed the intensity of the emotions on both sides. Perhaps Hayne did not know at the time that the Chief Justice had become a vice president of the ACS, but the Marshall-Madison appeal to the Virginia legislature for similar state funds had been given conspicuous publicity. Why was there no suggestion, by Hayne or other proslavery senators, of impeachment for such an attempt to destroy the Southern social and economic system? Presumably because the effects of the Chase acquittal were still dominant; congressional thought had not advanced to the state of mind exhibited by the political descendants of Senator Hayne.

In the campaign to impeach Justice Douglas for conduct similar to that of Chief Justice Marshall, the need of the Ford-Wyman-Waggonner alliance was to discover some action that contravened federal law. They thought they had it in the charge of practicing law while on the federal bench. Supporters of the principal accusation—that Douglas drafted the articles of incorporation of the Albert Parvin Foundation—had what looked at first like strong presumptive evidence. In 1963, Albert Parvin became engaged in litigation launched by his ex-wife, whom he had divorced with what was called "a very handsome settlement." In the Los Angeles Court of General Sessions, her lawyers began asking Parvin slurring questions about the foundation. The following exchange took place:

Q. This concern, we will call it, the Foundation, was incorporated under the laws of California, was it not?
A. I don't know.
Q. Well, did some lawyer advise you in connection with the setting up?
A. Oh, of course, of course.
Q. And who was the lawyer?
A. Well, the man that drafted the articles for the Foundation, William O. Douglas, Justice William O. Douglas, Robert Hutchins, and they in turn worked with Victor Mindlin . . . our company attorney for some time.

The statement was patently incorrect regarding Hutchins, head of the Santa Barbara Center for the Study of Democratic Institutions, who had no connection whatever with the Parvin Foundation until February 1, 1961, three months after its articles of incorporation were filed. In an affidavit to the special subcommittee, Victor Mindlin swore that the allegation concerning Justice Douglas "is completely untrue. I alone performed the legal work in drafting, preparing and filing the Articles of Incorporation and the By-Laws, as well as other steps incidental to setting up the Foundation." Justice Douglas had already denied it, saying, moreover, that he was not sufficiently acquainted with California law to be competent for such a task. Complete disproof was then found in the Douglas files which had been turned over to the Internal Revenue Service and to the special subcommittee:

Parvin to Douglas, at his summer home in Glenwood, Washington, September 9, 1960: "I am leaving for New York tomorrow and expect to be back on the West Coast Thursday. Upon my return I believe Victor Mindlin and Bob Spencer [Parvin's accountant] will have completed the draft of our incorporation papers. If so, I will send them to you for your perusal and comment."

Parvin to Douglas, September 19: "Mr. Mindlin, my attorney, has withheld filing of the corporate papers until the names of the directors and founders are established."

How did Parvin come to make his error? Presumably Douglas, as president-designate of the foundation, had given Mindlin an outline of its purposes and policies (an administrative action) for his use in drawing up the legal papers. The Celler subcommittee disposed of the contention in these words:

"The Special Subcommittee has examined the records of the Albert Parvin Foundation, the files of Albert Parvin, Justice Douglas, Robert Hutchins, Harry Ashmore [of the Santa Barbara Center], and the Internal Revenue Service. . . . The documentary materials obtained in this file examination show that Justice Douglas did not draft the

Articles of Incorporation of the Albert Parvin Foundation or provide legal service as its President."

Another charge of practicing law evolved from one of the foundation's most worthy projects—a campaign to combat illiteracy in the Dominican Republic after its escape from the oppressive Trujillo dictatorship.* With the election of Juan Bosch as president came the country's opportunity to restore constitutional government. Before his inauguration on February 27, 1963, Bosch asked Douglas to offer suggestions for safeguarding democracy in the proposed new constitution. In doing so, the justice also commented upon an agreement being sought by a Swiss consortium for an industrial development loan to the Dominican Republic.

To Representative Hutchinson of the special subcommittee this action looked like the practice of law, and he based his dissent from the subcommittee's report on it in large part. "The Justice," said he, "gave Bosch the same kind of advice a lawyer gives." What was the advice? That a fee amounting to 10 per cent of the entire loan, to be given to the negotiating agent, "is a whale of a big fee and I think utterly unconscionable." Also, said Douglas, the agent was hawking syndicate shares in American money circles, proving that he did not have complete Swiss banking support.

If such unsolicited free advice constitutes the practice of

---

*Our State Department strongly supported this program. The ambassador to the Dominican Republic, John Bartlow Martin, wrote on May 16, 1963, to Harry Ashmore, who helped set it up: "I am ever so grateful to you for the work you have done here. All of us are counting heavily on the Foundation program. In my opinion, as you know, this represents a perhaps unique opportunity to assist in building a democratic society on the wreckage of tyranny, an effort which, if it succeeds, will have importance far beyond the shores of this little island and further even beyond the Caribbean."

law, would the same advice from a professor of economics convict the professor of practicing law without a license? Chairman Celler and the subcommittee majority simply found that Douglas's comments on the contract were not "a provision of legal services or practicing law."

Less frivolous but equally without foundation was another reason for Hutchinson's dissent. He accepted in silence the conclusive proof that Douglas had no hand in the preparation of the Parvin Foundation articles of incorporation; but, he said, "it is evident that Mr. Parvin asked Justice Douglas for legal advice. Whether the Justice utterly renounced those requests for legal advice is debatable."

Search of the Parvin-Douglas correspondence possessed by the special subcommittee produces only two sentences that Hutchinson could possibly have construed as requests for legal advice. The first is in the Parvin letter of July 25, 1960, broaching the project of setting up the foundation: "Being a layman of limited capacities in such undertakings, I, therefore, seek your aid and advice." Aid and advice about what? About the feasibility of the undertaking. The other request is Parvin's statement of September 9, 1960, concerning the articles of incorporation: "I will send them to you for your perusal and comment." These trivialities are only important in measuring the difficulty Hutchinson had in finding any basis for his dissent.

Back in 1832, immediately following his election as vice president of the American Colonization Society, Chief Justice Marshall wrote to its national secretary, R. R. Gurley, regarding the future policies of the organization. The work had been carried on for sixteen years by private contributions. Now it was "of great importance to retain the countenance and protection of the General Government." For this he proposed a three-part program:

1. "Permanent laws" were needed by which the government would supply financial aid to the colonization project.

2. The unlawful importation of new slaves must be halted to prevent replacement of those who emigrated: "Some of our cruizers stationed on the Coast of Africa would, at the same time, interrupt the slave trade—a horrid traffic detested by all good men—and would protect the vessels and commerce of the colony [Liberia] from pirates who infest them. The power of the government to afford this aid is not, I believe, contested."

3. Use of the proceeds of public land sales to establish a colonization fund would be a good means—"the most effective that can be devised."

By the logic employed against Douglas, Marshall was clearly engaging in the practice of law. Moreover, in these statements he was passing judgment on constitutional issues of which some were being heatedly debated at the time, while others were certain to arise if the program he outlined was ever implemented by Congress. Even his statement that government power to use "cruizers" to halt the slave trade "is not, I believe, contested," meant only that it had not yet been contested. It surely would be if the elimination of slavery should come to depend on use of naval force for the particular purpose of its abolition—a goal not detectable in the enumerated or implied powers of Congress.

Today, use of proceeds from public land sales to promote the general welfare is universally regarded as constitutional, except for the mournful regrets of an occasional antediluvian senator. But long before and after 1832, furious debate raged over the question whether Congress had power to appropriate money to any object designed for the general welfare, or only to objects covered by the other enumerated powers. Chief Justice Marshall, by advocating public land sales to raise funds for manumission of slaves, committed himself to at least one of two legal propositions: that such sales and such use were permissible under the general welfare clause, or if not, that they were authorized by the power of Congress "to dispose of and make all needful regulations respecting" the public lands. Madison called this use of public land money the only practicable way to put an end to slavery.*

Actually, of course, Marshall was not practicing law when he formulated plans for the American Colonization Society, any more than Douglas was in the case of the Albert Parvin Foundation. There was no lawyer-client relationship, either paid or free, in their activities. But Marshall went far beyond Douglas by putting himself on record, not on insignificant matters remotely capable of reaching the Supreme Court, but on subjects that were then reverberating in congressional debate, and that were certain to reach the Court if the policies advocated by the Chief Justice were written into law.

The correspondence between the Chief Justice and Secretary Gurley was not known to Senator Hayne, but Marshall's sponsorship of the Liberian program was a public matter. Why did the proslavery forces hold their fire? Indeed, why had they not searched his record? What about the years when he was in sharp personal conflict with the Jefferson

---

* The notion of the Douglas impeachers that it is improper for a member of the Supreme Court to express himself on unsettled constitutional questions is contradicted by a huge volume of historical practice. Justice Joseph Story in his three-volume *Commentaries on the Constitution of the United States* (1833) stated his position on every constitutional issue he could think of—past, current, and future. His *Commentaries* are quoted today far more often than his judicial opinions. Justice Samuel F. Miller, the first Justice John M. Harlan, Chief Justice Charles Evans Hughes, and Justices Robert Jackson, Tom C. Clark, and Felix Frankfurter all were prolific writers and speakers who did not avoid controversial subjects while they sat on the Court.

administration, the years when his nationalistic decisions and opinions were anathema to all defenders of state sovereignty? Was there nothing under the rose or above it that could have been utilized by his political or ideological opponents as a ground of impeachment?

The single great cause of friction between John Marshall and Thomas Jefferson was Marshall's conduct in the treason proceedings against former Vice President Aaron Burr. Burr's 1805–6 plot to detach the Western states and territories from the United States ended in the collapse of his expedition as it floated down the Mississippi, and Burr himself was captured in the Mississippi Territory. Word reached Washington that Burr was being taken to Richmond, where Chief Justice Marshall was holding circuit court. Affidavits had to reach Richmond ahead of the prisoner or Marshall would release him on habeas corpus, as he had already done with two accused accomplices. Attorney General Caesar Rodney himself took horse to deliver the papers, but bad roads and hard riding broke him down in Fredericksburg. Hunting for a messenger, he found that Colonel William Tatham of Bowling Green was on his way to Richmond, but Tatham was too flighty to be trusted. He had, however, wrote Rodney, "a very faithful servant, I knew," so the precious papers were entrusted to the slave Joseph, who beat Burr to the state capital. The dramatic Rodney-Joseph relay illumines the depth of the Jeffersonians' distrust of Marshall.

Referring the case to the federal grand jury after heated argument, Marshall cut the charge against Burr from "treason" to "high misdemeanor," making a remark, in this connection, about "the hand of malignity." That could only mean the hand of Jefferson. On the evening following the Chief Justice's action, a great "victory dinner" was served at the home of Burr's chief counsel, John Wickham.

Knowing that Burr was to be the guest of honor, Chief Justice Marshall attended the dinner.

Biographer Albert Beveridge tried desperately to discount this occurrence, unimpeachably recorded by the eminent legal scholar James Thayer, Marshall's first biographer. Calling it "almost certainly a myth," Beveridge pointed to the lapse of time—a story that was not put on paper until 94 years (Beveridge said more than 100) after the dinner. But Thayer, born in Marshall's lifetime, was an intimate friend of the family who grew up with Marshall's children and grandchildren. He even recorded Mrs. Marshall's disregarded advice that her husband stay away from the affair.

Actually, Marshall's indiscreet action had no political significance. He and Wickham were close friends, and they alternately entertained the outstanding members of the Richmond bar. Their "lawyers' dinners" had statewide fame. So Marshall's presence at the dinner attracted no public attention. But what would have been the result if Jefferson had possessed the low ethical standards and malignity of the people who managed the campaign to impeach Justice Douglas? For that matter, what if the unconstitutional Chase impeachment had succeeded? Would not the conduct of the Chief Justice in the Burr episode, climaxed by the dinner, have been construed as impeachable?

To turn to the issue of dual employment, we find that on February 15, 1812, the Virginia general assembly passed an act appointing John Marshall and several others, any two of whom were to work with him, "to view James River" from Lynchburg up to the mouth of Dunlap's Creek. They were to "mark out the best and most direct way for a turnpike road" over the mountains to the highest waters leading into the Ohio River that could be made navigable. They were also to study these western rivers and report the expense and probable advantage of making them navigable. For that task, including the preparation of a report to the legislature which Marshall wrote unaided, the legislature appropriated $750 as expense money.

This was a trivial sum by modern standards, and it was for a task that Marshall was delighted to perform. He had a zest for camping and surveying that was equal, certainly, to the nonjudicial energy Justice Douglas had put into mountain climbing. In comparison with Marshall's $4,000 salary as Chief Justice, however, $750 was not inconsequential.

Yet it never seemed to have occurred to Marshall or anyone else that, having received a modest stipend from his state, he should disqualify himself four years later in *Cohens v. Virginia*. With no more reason, the issue of failure to disqualify himself was raised in 1970 against Justice Douglas. A federal statute on that subject reads:

"Any justice or judge of the United States shall disqualify himself in any case in which he has a substantial interest, has been of counsel, is or has been a material witness, or is so related to or connected with any party or his attorney as to render it improper, in his opinion, for him to sit on the trial, appeal, or other proceeding therein."

Representative Ford accused Justice Douglas of violating this law and outlined the following sequence of events: Early in 1967 a New York federal jury awarded Senator Barry Goldwater $75,000 for libel by a magazine, *Fact*, owned by Ralph Ginzburg. The March 1969 issue of *Avant Garde*, a second Ginzburg magazine, contained an article by Justice Douglas on "The Appeal of Folk Singing," for which he was paid $350. Four months later the United States Court of Appeals affirmed the award to Senator Goldwater. On January 26, 1970, the Supreme Court denied Ginzburg's petition for a review of the Goldwater decision. Justice Black dissented on the ground that freedom of the press is absolute, and Justice Douglas joined in

Black's dissent. Representatives Ford and Wyman contended that the failure of Justice Douglas to disqualify himself, after receiving $350 for his *Avant Garde* article, was an impeachable departure from good behavior. The justice should have known, when he submitted his article to *Avant Garde*, that the case concerning *Fact* was "clearly headed for the highest court in the land."

The special subcommittee found documentary proof "that on January 13, 1969, when he submitted the article, Justice Douglas did not know and had no reason to believe that Mr. Ginzburg or *Fact* was related to *Avant Garde*." (He learned this on February 28, from a *New York Times* reporter.) Mixing law and horse sense, the subcommittee threw out the whole accusation. To know that a case was "clearly headed for the highest Court," the Justice would need to be acquainted with more than one hundred thousand cases which at all times are pending in the lower federal courts. Yet even if he had known all the facts in the Ginzburg case, there would have been no reason for him to disqualify himself. Said the subcommittee:

"Existence of knowledge of the relationship is not the test of disqualification. 28 U.S.C. 455 requires disqualification if there is a substantial interest in a case, or a relation or connection, that, in the justice's opinion made it improper for him to continue to sit. The $350 payment certainly is *de minimus* [the law takes no account of trifles] and the relationship between Justice Douglas and Ralph Ginzburg was virtually nonexistent. Clearly it was not extensive, not intimate, not continuing and failure to disqualify was not improper."*

---

* 28 U.S.C. 455, an extraordinary law requiring each justice to disqualify himself for relations which *in his opinion* (and his alone) require it, was lobbied through Congress in a period (1848) when Supreme Court feuds were intense. It had been initiated by one member of the Court as a slap at

In light of the stew over Douglas's participation in the Ginzburg case, involving a common ownership of magazines about which he had no knowledge, consider the circumstances in *Mason* v. *Wilson*, 1 Cranch 44, decided in 1801. Chief Justice Marshall wrote the opinion, overthrowing a decision of the Kentucky Supreme Court in a land speculation contest. The winning lawyer (and undercover land claimant) was Joseph H. Daveiss, who shortly afterward married the sister of the Chief Justice. Possibly, of course, his was a whirlwind courtship; but what would Douglas's prospects of survival have been if anything like this had been discovered about him?

The theoretical impeachability of Chief Justice Marshall vanishes into thin air at every point, except as the aims and methods of the Douglas prosecutors are applied to it. Equally striking in that respect is the similarity of *purpose* but contrast in *methods* between the attempt of President Jefferson to get rid of Justice Chase and the campaign of the modern "remakers of the Court" to eliminate Justice Douglas.

Jefferson set the House Managers on Chase, but virtually every factual accusation they made against him was demonstrably true. The fallacy was that they treated those facts as constitutional grounds of impeachment. In sharp contrast, the prosecutors of Justice Douglas resorted to false

a fellow member who (quite properly) failed to disqualify himself in a case argued by a onetime law partner with whom he had had no business relations or personal contact for more than twenty years. The only effect of this meaningless, unnecessary law has been to prevent the sons of Supreme Court justices from moving out of law school into apprentice positions with large law firms. The presence of one such apprentice among 150 lawyers would force a disqualification that might cause the firm to lose a case in a four-to-four division of the Court. If the law is ever repealed, one justice remarked to this author a few years ago, the initiative will have to come from outside the Court.

accusations, fallacious interpretations, and reckless innuendoes. Consider the course of the only nontrivial impeachable charge: that Douglas drafted the articles of incorporation of the Albert Parvin Foundation.

Following up the publicity given to this and the related accusations, the Internal Revenue Service in 1966 began an inquiry into the personal affairs of Albert Parvin and the functioning of the Parvin Foundation. Two IRS agents called on Douglas to inquire about the foundation's inception and purposes. He told them, they said in their report, that he had nothing to do with drafting the articles of incorporation, and opened his files to them. They took copies of letters showing that the work was done solely by Victor Mindlin and Robert Spencer.

After investigating all charges that Albert Parvin was linked with organized crime, special agents Vernon E. Lynch and Peter W. Greene said in their final report on April 21, 1967: "The specific allegations have been found to be baseless," and the nonspecific charges (chiefly of income tax evasion) had been pursued far enough to indicate "that a continuation of this sampling would lead only to further negative results." To investigate a charge that the Parvin Foundation was utilized in "fostering a liberal attitude in officials of emergent countries toward gambling," the agents had examined all books and records, canceled checks, bank deposits and statements, and minutes of corporate meetings, and had conducted numerous interviews. "No evidence was found indicating that Mr. Parvin utilized the Albert Parvin Foundation as alleged." They recommended that "this case be closed," both in its criminal and civil aspects, but that the investigation of the foundation's tax-exempt status be continued by the audit division as a civil item.

The foundation, on the initiative of Douglas, retained

one of the leading tax lawyers of the United States, Carolyn Agger (the wife of Douglas's colleague, Justice Abe Fortas) of Arnold and Porter, Washington, D.C. She studied the records, consulted the IRS, and reported the charges to be "picayune." After three years of work, the audit division had not completed its inquiry when the special subcommittee closed its investigation of the Douglas charges in September 1970. In the meantime, on April 17, 1969, the Internal Revenue Service sent a notice to the Parvin Foundation which was even more astounding for its wording than for its substance. It was a notification that the IRS intended to revoke the foundation's income tax exemption in thirty days. The charges began:

"At the time of incorporation of the Foundation, Mr. Parvin was arranging with the Princeton University Press for the commercial publication of a paperback edition of the book 'America Challenged,' authored by Justice William O. Douglas who had drafted the articles of the foundation and had assisted in rendering legal advice to Mr. Parvin regarding the formation of the foundation."

The charge concerning the paperback edition—that the foundation subsidized it for the financial benefit of Justice Douglas—was later analyzed and found to be false by the special subcommittee.* But why did the Internal Revenue Service implant the greater falsehood (which it knew to be a lie) that the justice "drafted the articles of the foundation"? Agents of the IRS had themselves selected letters from the Douglas files disproving this charge. Their report recommending dismissal of all criminal and civil charges

---

* The subcommittee found that the purpose of paperback publication was "to disseminate the book." Incidental royalties went to Douglas "in order partially to compensate him for hardcover royalties . . . that would inevitably be lost as a result of the competing paperback sales." Any author can confirm this experience.

had been approved. Finally, the drafting of the articles of incorporation was completely irrelevant to the tax status of the foundation—the only subject with which the IRS was still concerned.

The sole conceivable purpose was to plant, in a seemingly casual manner, an assertion which if true would furnish a technical ground of impeachment. What had happened between April 17, 1967, when IRS agents gave Douglas and the foundation a clean bill of health on the trumped-up charges, and April 14, 1969, when, without waiting for conclusion of the tax inquiry, the IRS took action on it? In doing so, why did it inject this false and irrelevant charge of impeachable conduct? What changes had taken place that could account for the extraordinary shift of attitude and policy?

Richard Milhous Nixon had been elected President of the United States, with his first priority the "remaking" of the Supreme Court to fit his political philosophy. And the Commissioner of Internal Revenue had resigned from this political office immediately after the election.

A second charge in the 1969 IRS impeachment drive against Douglas was as specious as the first. The Parvin Foundation entered into a contract with Justice Douglas by which, in accordance with IRS regulations, $2,400 was deducted each year from his salary, tax-free, to set up a retirement annuity. The tax lawyer who drew up the contract was Sheldon Cohen, who, shortly afterward became general counsel of the IRS and subsequently Commissioner. It was he who resigned to allow President Nixon to appoint a Republican. Concerning this contract, the IRS under new management now said in its notice of termination of exemption:

"In addition, the foundation paid a $2,400 premium on a retirement annuity for Justice Douglas. Of this amount,

$1,400 was entered on the foundation's records as an account receivable. This was an unsecured, non-interest bearing indebtedness owed to the foundation by its president."

In reality, the foundation's so-called recording of that "account receivable" was simply a way of putting its books in balance. Owing to the date at which the contract was signed, $1,400 of the deduction from 1961 salary had to be taken out in 1962. The entire concoction was exactly what Justice Douglas privately called it: "a manufactured case . . . to get me off the Court."

Following the change in IRS control, there was a great upsurge in newspaper publicity adverse to Douglas, the Parvin Foundation, and the Center for the Study of Democratic Institutions. Many of the details duplicated the materials that had been turned over to the special subcommittee when it applied to the IRS and the Justice Department for everything in their possession bearing on the Douglas case. Included were allegations of Douglas's connection with organized crime and gambling—the sort of charges that were called baseless in the 1967 report by IRS agents but that were played to the hilt in Ford's impeachment speech. The subcommittee ran these stories down, interviewed every person named in them (not one of them knew Douglas), and summed up its findings:

"The Special Subcommittee has no evidence that Justice Douglas was involved in any way, directly or indirectly, with organized crime."*

---

* These charges began in 1966, when efforts were made to connect the Parvin Foundation with the owners of the Flamingo Hotel (now part of the Hilton-Sheraton chain) during the time before Parvin bought it and the period after he sold it. Criticism was intensified by the Parvin-Dohrmann Company's purchase, on July 1, 1966, of the Fremont Hotel in Las Vegas. On learning in the press of the transaction, Douglas urged Parvin to keep the foundation "clear of any Las Vegas investment" and undertook to get rid of this one. Regulations of the Securities and Exchange Commission, which

Ford's guilt-by-association campaign reached its zenith in an attempt to link Douglas with Bobby Baker, the one-time influential drum major of the Senate Democratic caucus, who became a financial go-go-getter and landed in the federal penitentiary. The principal evidence presented was that during a six-month period in which Douglas made several trips to Santo Domingo to further the foundation's campaign against illiteracy, Baker too visited the island several times in an unsuccessful attempt to secure a casino concession. The subcommittee obtained documentary proof that both men were never in Santo Domingo at the same time.

To establish that there were links between them, Ford charged that both men, presumably together, attended the inauguration of the Dominican Republic's President Bosch. The truth is that Baker did so; Douglas, although invited to attend, remained in Washington. Finally Baker lost his casino bid, whereupon, Ford claimed, "the further interest of the Albert Parvin Foundation in the Dominican Republic abruptly ceased." The special subcommittee presented documentary proof that the foundation continued its campaign against illiteracy until President Bosch was overthrown, and tried to resume it under his successor.

The climax of the charges linking Justice Douglas with Baker came in Ford's statement: "On October 22, 1962, Bobby Baker turned up in Las Vegas for a 3-day stay. . . . On Baker's registration card a hotel employee had noted—'is with Douglas.'" Ford offered no surmises concerning their common objectives; he had no need to do so. The words "Bobby Baker"—"is with Douglas"—"in Las Vegas"

---

classified Parvin as a "control person" in Parvin-Dohrmann, prevented sale of the foundation's P-D stock, except a small fraction at a time, until 1969. In that year Parvin sold his own holdings in Parvin-Dohrmann, thus clearing the way for sale by the foundation.

—carried mountainous implications of a nefarious plot in organized gambling. With apparent generosity of spirit, Ford conceded that the wording " '*is* with Douglas' . . . left it unclear whether the note meant literally that Mr. Justice Douglas was also visiting Las Vegas at that time or whether it meant only to identify Baker as a Douglas associate."

The special subcommittee, after more than two months of pounding, finally obtained from Attorney General John Mitchell a copy of Bobby Baker's motel reservation card, which had been so readily turned over to Representative Ford. The subcommittee's report discloses three things wrong with Mr. Ford's description of the incident:

1. The motel was located in Beverly Hills, California, not in Las Vegas.

2. The clerk's notation on the card did not read "is with Douglas." It read "with Douglas move 176–7," an obvious reference to somebody named Douglas, connected with Baker, who was to be moved from or into suite 176–7.

3. During the three days when Bobby Baker was at the motel, Justice Douglas was in the Republic of Chile.

The incident throws as clear a light on Attorney General Mitchell, in relation to the attempt to remove Justice Douglas from the Supreme Court, as its does on Minority Leader Ford. The special subcommittee made no specific accusation, but it singled out this incident to illustrate the uncooperative attitude of the Attorney General. Still more revealing are the general comments in the subcommittee report, recounting efforts that extended from June 9 to September 16, 1970, to obtain pertinent information and documentary material from the Justice Department. After weeks of negotiation, the subcommittee succeeded in obtaining summaries of documents and reports containing "numerous unverified allegations, rumors, reports from unidentified confidential informants, and other information of questionable evidentiary value." For another month the department refused access to the documents themselves; then, on August 6, it laid down "ground rules." The subcommittee's staff "could examine the documents, but could not make notes, and no copies of documents would be furnished." These terms were rejected, to avoid implied acceptance of undue "executive privilege" to withhold information relative to impeachment proceedings.

"Most noteworthy," says the report of the subcommittee, "is the failure to supply documents and materials in the Department of Justice files which evaluate the charges and incidents described in the FBI summaries . . . [which include] rumors and hearsay, from a variety of sources of unknown reliability." In the end, the Justice Department delivered a total of thirty-six documents, "including the Baker hotel records."

Considering the ease with which Ford obtained unevaluated material from the Justice Department to use against Douglas, it seems unlikely that the refusal to furnish the special subcommittee with FBI evaluations of this material was due to a desire to protect Douglas. The FBI, when it picked up the registration card, was investigating a lawyer who paid Bobby Baker's motel bill. Is it conceivable that the agents neglected or failed to identify the "Douglas" who moved in or out of suite 176–7? Was he not identified in the evaluated report? The special subcommittee summed up its experience:

"The cooperation of the Department of Justice falls far short of what the Special Subcommittee could reasonably expect from the principal investigative arm of the Executive Branch."

The subcommittee's relations with the Internal Revenue Service were a little better but far from satisfactory. Here the need was to run down and evaluate a mass of rumor and hearsay furnished by the IRS concerning alleged criminal activities involving either the Parvin Foundation or Justice Douglas. The special subcommittee reported:

"Reference to organized crime connections and associations with underworld characters, as related to the operations of the Albert Parvin Foundation or to the activities of Justice Douglas that are found in the IRS materials are acknowledged [by the IRS] to be based on coincidence of events, hypothetical speculation, and on newspaper accounts. . . . The Special Subcommittee reiterates its finding that nothing in Committee's files of this investigation supports these charges."

The subcommittee found, however, that the newspaper stories traveled a two-way street. Without comment, the report presented evidence that such material was fed to the press by the IRS itself. It published a letter (of June 12, 1969) to Justice Douglas from John L. Perry, president of the Center for the Study of Democratic Institutions: Several newspaper friends, Perry said, had told him that it "apparently is a rather well-established policy by the Internal Revenue Service of 'leaking' information from government tax files to the press."

Three Washington newsmen, Perry went on, had lately confirmed this. A reporter for *Life* Magazine, one of the trio told him, was frequently so "loaded down by the IRS with 'leaked' information . . . that his constant problem is how to write his stories in such a way as to give the impression that he receives the information from non-IRS sources." Another letter quoted in the report was by Harry E. Ashmore, who was secretary of the Santa Barbara Center at the time.

"On the day the press was making a big issue out of the expense fees and honoraria paid to you by the Center," wrote Ashmore to Justice Douglas on June 16, 1969, reporter James Polk of the Associated Press called him from Washington. "He rattled off figures on payments through 1967, and then asked if I could give him the amount for 1968."

Ashmore asked, "Why don't you get these figures where you got the others?"

"The IRS is sending the files down from Philadelphia, and they haven't gotten here yet," Polk replied.

The postelection conduct of the Justice Department and the Internal Revenue Service epitomizes the entire drive to remove Justice Douglas from the Supreme Court in order to make way for a member with a different concept of the rights and liberties embodied in the Constitution. The whole record reveals the ease with which the modern miracles of communications can be employed by government to accomplish its purposes, and in the process to mislead newspapers, radio, and television. The use to which executive power was put in 1970 to attack Douglas forms a menacing contrast to the immunity of Chief Justice Marshall from similar action against him during his ideological conflicts with Presidents and with political factions in Congress and the states.

CHAPTER VI

PECK AND HUMPHREYS

Following the acquittal of Justice Chase, a quarter century elapsed before another impeachment was voted by the House of Representatives. On May 11, 1830, the Senate took up charges against James H. Peck, United States judge for the district of Missouri. Judge Peck, encountering criticism of his decision against a claim to public lands by the Soulard family, had published his opinion in a St. Louis newspaper. The losing litigant's lawyer, Luke E. Lawless, countered with an article in the same paper specifying eighteen legal errors in the opinion and challenging the judge's recollection of the lawyer's argument. Peck found Lawless guilty of contempt of court, sent him to prison for twenty-four hours, and suspended him from practicing in federal court for eighteen months.

Peck was impeached for this action, which was alleged to have been taken with criminal intent. He was acquitted, 21 to 22—eight votes short of the required two thirds. The case was noteworthy only for the opinions that developed concerning the constitutional grounds of impeachment.

The House Managers leveled their opening fire against the most extreme position taken by counsel for Justice Chase—that a judge was subject to removal only for committing some indictable high crime or misdemeanor. Manager Ambrose Spencer of New York contended that a judge could be impeached for "doing an illegal act," under the cloak of his office, that was committed with bad motives, or for an act within his competency, unwarranted by the existing facts, that was committed with bad motives. This was substantially in accord with the Senate's verdict in the Chase trial. Judge Peck was acquitted because of the prosecution's failure to prove evil intent, which was in effect a decision that he had not violated his oath of office. House Manager Charles A. Wickliffe of Kentucky echoed Spencer's argument regarding indictable offenses and went considerably farther, taking a position that seemed to combine those of Caesar Rodney and Joseph Nicholson in the Chase trial. "I maintain the proposition," said he, "that any official act committed or omitted by the judge, which is a violation of the condition upon which he holds his office, is an impeachable offense under the Constitution." By the words "condition upon which he holds his office," he seemed to mean tenure "during good behavior."

Accordingly, Wickliffe rejected the construction that (as he phrased it) no conduct would be impeachable "unless it be a high crime and misdemeanor, within the technical meaning of these terms, and punishable by some known and existing criminal law." By avoiding such crimes, a degraded judge "covered with disgrace and immorality, [would] smile with contempt at your power, and shield himself under the imputed ignorance of the members of the convention."

Wickliffe's interpretation would subject any judge to

removal for anything the Senate chose to regard as "maladministration." He proposed in effect to amend the Constitution by construction, in order to remedy the ignorance of the framers. However, it was not through ignorance of potential judicial misconduct but through knowledge of senatorial frailties that the framers had rejected maladministration. They saw more to fear in "tenure during the pleasure of the Senate" than in noncriminal misconduct by judges.

Wickliffe then took up the mandatory provision for removal from office. The framers acted wisely, he said, when they limited punishment to removal from office and disqualification to hold office in the future. An offender might deserve both punishments or only one—or perhaps neither. "A reprimand, a temporary suspension of his functions and salary, might, in particular cases, be a punishment equal to the official misdemeanor." If the Senate possessed such latitude, it might through humanity, mercy, or even evil purpose impose only a reprimand on a judge or other officer who was "stained with the foul crime of treason and bribery, or other high crimes and misdemeanors." To prevent this, they commanded that all officers so impeached and convicted "shall be removed from office. . . . This language is imperative; it leaves you no discretion; you can not stop short of removal from office, you can not exceed it."

Wickliffe's reasoning about the meaning of the mandatory provision was irrefutable. It differed vastly from Manager Bayard's contention in the Blount trial that "shall be removed" merely specified the minimum punishment of President, Vice President, and civil officers, leaving the House and Senate free to impeach private citizens, with the same punishment.

To illustrate the application of his concept of impeachment, Wickliffe set forth hypothetical cases involving

offenses not subject to indictment. Suppose a judge, influenced by political feeling, should award his favorite a new
trial "against known law." Suppose a President should veto
every act which Congress should pass. Suppose a head of a
department should direct his official "power and patronage,
not to the promotion of the welfare of his country, but with
the known and avowed purpose of his own personal or
political aggrandizement."

In any of these instances, Wickliffe asked, "Who would
think of finding an indictment in a criminal court of justice
against him? Yet who would not remove him from office by
impeachment?" If precedent was to rule, he thought, the
case was settled by the Senate's conviction of Judge Pickering for "disregard of a plain statute of the United States"
in disposing of an admiralty case. The judge's alcoholism,
though a misdemeanor, had never been denominated a
"high misdemeanor" by the laws of any country.

Wickliffe's illustrations formed a potpourri of completely
different types of cases. His imaginary examples of misconduct by the judge and the President amounted to violations
of their oath of office. Judge Pickering's alleged violation of
admiralty law, however, was an excuse to get rid of him for
reasons of political affiliation and alcoholic incompetence.
By their elastic inclusiveness, the illustrations muddled
Wickliffe's contention that a judge may be removed for any
violation of "the condition upon which he holds his office"
—to wit, "good behavior."

The argument for Judge Peck's liability was taken up by
Manager James Buchanan, whose standing as a lawyer was
considerably higher than his rank among the Presidents of
the United States. He opened with a concession that aligned
him with Robert Goodloe Harper of the Chase defense
battery and put him squarely in opposition to Wickliffe, to
the prosecutors of Chase, and to the men who in the

twentieth century sought to impeach Justice Douglas:

"I freely admit that we are bound to prove that the respondent has violated the Constitution or some known law of the land. This, I think, was the principle fairly to be deduced from all the arguments on the trial of Judge Chase, and from the votes of the Senate in the articles of impeachment against him."

The principle he expounded, Buchanan noted, was opposed to the Chase counsel's original argument that "to render an offense impeachable it must be indictable." However, it was Buchanan's opinion that "this violation of law may consist in the abuse, as well as in the usurpation of Authority." Suppose a man were found guilty of ordinary assault and battery. If the judge should fine him a thousand dollars and commit him to prison for a year, would not such a tyrannical and arbitrary exercise of power justify impeachment?

This example, Buchanan declared, was truly analogous to the charge against Judge Peck. Counsel for the judge had "labored for hours" to prove that the "perfectly decorous" article by lawyer Lawless was a libel. It imputed no criminal intention to the judge in his ruling on the land claim. Even admitting the power of the judge to punish Lawless, was it not "a cruel and oppressive use of authority" to degrade the author of the article by imprisonment and by depriving him of the means of earning bread for himself and his family for eighteen months? Buchanan took this stand:

"A gross abuse of granted power and an usurpation of power not granted are offenses equally worthy of and liable to impeachment."

The charge against Judge Peck, Buchanan declared, was not merely that he had made an illegal decision on a question of property; it was that he had committed an act which was in itself criminal. "In an arbitrary and oppressive manner, and without the authority of law," he had imprisoned a citizen of this country and thus consigned him to infamy. Did not the act itself—"the product of a jaundiced mind and wounded vanity"—permit the inference of criminal intent?

Peck's defense was managed by William Wirt, the noted libertarian lawyer and biographer of Patrick Henry, who had just ended twelve years' service as Attorney General in the administrations of Presidents Monroe and John Quincy Adams. Wirt emphatically rejected Buchanan's inference that his client had acted in an arbitrary and oppressive manner. Peck was "innocent and simple-hearted as a child, . . . amiable, patient, and forbearing." Peck might have made an error, but Wirt had "yet to learn that such an error would be a high misdemeanor in the sense of the Constitution of the United States." Wirt put heavy emphasis on the absence of criminal intent:

"Even if the judge were proved to have mistaken the law, that would not warrant a conviction unless the guilt of intention be also established. For a mere mistake of the law is no crime or misdemeanor in a judge. It is the intention that is the essence of every crime."

The Managers who prepared the articles of impeachment had recognized this fact, said Wirt, for the articles expressly charged criminal intention. In argument, however, they implicitly confessed their inability to prove such an intention by contending that if they could prove the commission of an unlawful act, "the guilty intention charged in the impeachment followed as a necessary implication of law. This I deny; for then every mistake of law on the part of a judge would become a crime or a civil injury, for which he would be personally responsible."

Finally, Wirt took up a New York State habeas corpus

proceeding that furnished a close analogy to impeachment. The decision came from one of the most renowned American legal scholars, Chief Justice James Kent of the New York Supreme Court, whose published works include two casebooks on impeachments in state courts. In 1808, John Van Ness Yates, a master in chancery, filed a lawsuit in the name of another attorney without his knowledge or consent. Chancellor John Lansing, titular head of the New York judiciary, imprisoned Yates for contempt of court, declaring that such papers required the consent of the attorney whose name was used. Yates's attorney, the eminent Irish-American Thomas Addis Emmet, applied to the New York Supreme Court for release of his client on a writ of habeas corpus directed against Chancellor Lansing.*

It was an extraordinary confrontation. Chief Justice Kent ranked second to Chancellor Lansing in the New York judicial "pecking order" (and actually succeeded him in the chancellorship), but Kent's court was superior in jurisdiction. Mr. Wirt dealt at length with Kent's opinion:†

"What," asked Wirt, "does the judge declare to be an impeachable offense? The acting with knowledge (scienter) that the judge was violating the law—'the intentional violation of the law.'" As Wirt recorded Kent's opinion:

"The chancellor, he says, was bound to imprison the party if he considered his conduct as a contempt of court. He might have been mistaken in considering that as a contempt, which in truth was not one. But this would have been a mere error of judgment, for which he was not

---

* This case involved a breach in family friendships. John Van Ness Yates was the son of Robert Yates, copartner of John Lansing as delegates to the Federal Convention of 1787. Representing Governor George Clinton's New York State Rights political machine, they went home when they found themselves unable to perpetuate the old Articles of Confederation.

† His paraphrase of it was reprinted by the special subcommittee in the case of Justice Douglas.

answerable either civilly much less criminally. If he knew that it was not a contempt, and still punished it as one, it would have been an intentional violation of the law, which would have been an impeachable offense."

Wirt applied Kent's reasoning to the case of Judge Peck. "Here," he said, "is the very doctrine for which we are contending—that it is the guilty intention which forms the gist of the charge in every impeachment, and that a mere mistake of judgment is not an impeachable offense." Wirt said he had carefully examined "the various cases of impeachment of judges, both in England and the United States, and I have not observed that any counsel, even under the severest stress of the evidence, has taken refuge in so bold a proposition as this which we are considering—that error of judgment is an impeachable offense."

The Senate agreed and acquitted Judge Peck, whose action and behavior had been arbitrary, oppressive, unfair, petulant, and violative of freedom of the press. But he had not intentionally violated the law and therefore had not violated his oath of office. Consequently he had not committed a "high misdemeanor." Thus the acquittal of Peck gave added force to the acquittal of Chase, in repelling the early efforts of House Managers to extend the power of impeachment by reading into it the excesses of British practice, which the framers of the Constitution attempted to forestall.

Thirty years went by before the House of Representatives passed another impeachment resolution. This time the candidate was made to order for conviction—West W. Humphreys, judge of the United States Court for the district of Tennessee, who joined the Southern Confederacy upon the outbreak of the Civil War, abandoned his duties as a United States judge, and accepted a judgeship under the Confederate states.

Judge Humphreys was clearly guilty of treason, even by the narrow definition of that crime in the Constitution, that it "shall consist only in levying war against [the United States], or in adhering to their enemies, giving them aid and comfort." He did both, with overt acts every day to prove it. He was equally liable to impeachment for violating his oath of office by deliberately refusing to hold court under the United States. But instead of confining the accusations to these clearly demonstrable grounds of impeachment, the House of Representatives set forth a series of actions, some of them prior to the outbreak of fighting, culminating in acts of treason without the use of that word to describe them. The articles gave these reasons for impeachment:

1. For advocating secession in a public speech at Nashville, December 29, 1860.

2. For openly supporting and advocating the Tennessee ordinance of secession.

3. For aid in organizing armed rebellion.

4. For conspiring with Jefferson Davis and others to oppose by force the authority of the government of the United States.

5. For neglecting and refusing to hold the district court of the United States.

6. and 7. For acting as a Confederate judge.

Judge Humphreys was impeached, removed from office, and disqualified to hold any future position of trust, honor, or profit under the United States. He offered no defense, either in person or by attorney. The Senate convicted him separately on each of the seven counts, giving no consideration to their relative adequacy as constitutional grounds of impeachment.

This mixing of good and bad grounds of impeachment reversed a strict construction of the Constitution that had prevailed for more than half a century. The product of impulse springing from the Civil War, it was seized on to justify the next and far more drastic attack on constitutional limitations—the impeachment of President Andrew Johnson in 1868. Said Representative William Lawrence of New York, in a brief presented by the House Managers of the Johnson trial:

"The Senate [in the Humphreys case] by a separate vote on each article, specifically passed on the sufficiency of each article to constitute an impeachable offense, while a jury passes generally on all the counts of an indictment. And it is to be observed that the report of the Judiciary Committee recommending impeachment did not charge treason or other indictable crime, nor was there evidence of any; and on the trial of the case no doubt was expressed as to the right to convict on each of the articles."

This was a thoroughly disingenuous argument. Of course there was no dissent and no discussion. Humphreys offered no defense. Twenty-two Southern senators were absent. Those seeking impeachment, having solid grounds of conviction on five articles, were not going to diminish the appearance of Union solidarity by a dispute over two other articles that could not affect the outcome of the trial. Omission of the word "treason" was without significance: the indictment charged conduct that was within the constitutional definition of treason.

Suppose the Southern states had failed to secede, thus eliminating five articles of impeachment. Would Judge Humphreys have been impeached for delivering a speech futilely advocating secession? If impeached for this alone, with the Senate at full membership, would the judge have been convicted and removed from office without a single senator, Southern or Northern, raising the issue of freedom of speech? It is inconceivable.

Yet the lapse of senatorial judgment that took place in

the Humphreys case, stimulated by the high emotions of the moment, has helped in calmer periods to build up a chronic and menacing movement in House and Senate to subvert the safeguards of responsible government implanted in the Constitution. That effort has been, and still is, to pattern impeachment on what it was in Stuart England—an instrument of monarchic misuse of power over submissive Parliaments, or of parliamentary warfare against oppressive kings. To the men who framed our Constitution, that period did not lie in remote antiquity; it was yesterday.

CHAPTER VII

THE JOHNSON TRIAL:
ATTAINDER BY
IMPEACHMENT

THE IMPEACHMENT TRIAL of President Andrew Johnson presented a strange phenomenon that has gone unnoticed in histories. Besides rebutting the specific charges against him, Johnson's counsel assailed the impeachment as a violation of the Constitution. By the nature of those charges, they contended, the proceeding violated the clause forbidding Congress to pass bills of attainder. Lawyer after lawyer hammered on that theme, but not once did a House Manager reply. The reason appears obvious: they regarded silence as a better strategy than unconvincing denials.

What is a bill of attainder? The Supreme Court defined it in the very year of the Johnson impeachment, when the Court struck down two laws passed at the close of the Civil War that required lawyers and clergymen to take loyalty oaths as a precondition to practicing their profession. Said the Court in *Cummings* v. *Missouri*, holding the oath for lawyers to be in violation of the Constitution:

"A bill of attainder is a legislative act which inflicts

punishment without a judicial trial. If the punishment be less than death, the act is termed a bill of pains and penalties. Within the meaning of the Constitution, bills of attainder include bills of pains and penalties."

In the modern world, bills of attainder never bear either that name or the lesser one. To label them as such in the United States would automatically stamp them as unconstitutional. They have to be identified by analysis. They need not even take the form of actual legislative bills. Any action by both houses of Congress, or by either house, or by any legislative committee, which inflicts punishment without a judicial trial—that is, without a trial in a court of law—is a bill of attainder within the meaning of the Constitution. Rightly construed, the impeachment process must fall within the category of attainder if conviction results from charges not sanctioned by the Constitution.*

President Andrew Johnson did many things that invited the wrath of a Congress gripped by deep emotions after four years of civil war. Johnson, a Tennessee senator who opposed the secession of his state and adhered to the Union throughout the war, was given the vice presidential nomination in 1864 out of gratitude and party policy. The assassination of President Lincoln thrust him into the Presidency on April 15, 1865, at the moment of transition from war to peace, from preservation of the Union to the difficult and complex task of restoring national government and national unity.

---

* The author of this book reached that conclusion regarding impeachment as attainder before studying the Johnson trial. For attainder by congressional committees, see his address at the 1954 annual dinner of the Columbia University Law Review, published in condensed form in the *New Republic*, December 20, 1954, under the title "Sentence First, Verdict Afterwards," and in a different condensation, as a pamphlet by the Emergency Civil Liberties Committee of New York City, entitled *Congressional Investigations and Bills of Attainder*.

The immediate question was: Should the eleven Confederate states be regarded as still legally part of the Union, and treated as if they never had left it? Or should they be regarded as conquered provinces, to be readmitted as states under such conditions as Congress should prescribe and they should agree to? President Johnson took the former view; Congress the latter. Each side invoked the name of Abraham Lincoln, but Lincoln's final policies put him much closer to the views of his successor than to those of the Radical Republican leadership in Congress.

On the crucial issue of "rebel suffrage" there were three successive postwar policies. In reorganizing Arkansas, Louisiana, Tennessee, and Virginia, Lincoln as commander in chief disfranchised only Confederate leaders. President Johnson, ruling alone in the April–December 1865 absence of Congress, extended the disfranchisement to Confederate generals and men owning property worth more than $20,000. His object was to let poor whites govern the South and to break up the big plantations. The Radical Republicans in Congress demanded full enfranchisement of the former slaves who, under the Johnson plan already in effect, were being held close to their former status.

In the Congress that convened in December 1865, Representative Thaddeus Stevens of Pennsylvania rose swiftly to leadership of the radicals by virtue of his personal drive and the intensity of his convictions. In the Senate Charles Sumner of Massachusetts, a veteran abolitionist, gained similar preeminence. In swift succession, over the President's veto, Congress passed a series of Reconstruction Acts largely designed to protect the black population. From the Radical Republicans also came the historic Thirteenth, Fourteenth, and Fifteenth Amendments, which, as far as infringement by state action is concerned, now form the bedrock of liberty and equality under the law for all

American citizens and particularly safeguard Negro rights. To enforce the Reconstruction laws, the states of the late Confederacy were divided into military districts ruled by Union troops.

Trouble mounted between Johnson and Congress. In the Cabinet, Secretary of War Edwin Stanton vigorously opposed the President's Reconstruction policies. Word spread that Stanton was to be asked to resign. Congress quickly passed "an Act regulating the tenure of certain offices," which became law (again over Presidential veto) on March 2, 1867. By its terms the President could not remove any head of department without the prior consent of the Senate.

This law was patently unconstitutional. The President's power to remove such officers without consent of the Senate was debated at length in 1789 and thoroughly established by a declaratory act of Congress, not conferring that authority but worded to recognize its existence as an exclusive constitutional power. Madison, the first to champion this principle, called it "absolutely necessary" that the President should have the power of removing such officers. "It will make him in a peculiar manner responsible for their conduct, and subject him to impeachment himself if he suffers them to perpetrate . . . crimes . . . or neglects to superintend their conduct so as to check their excesses."

Thus, as he did later in the same speech (described in Chapter I), Madison coupled the removal power of the President with the obligations of his oath of office. Countering the plausible but superficial argument that the Senate, because its consent was required in the appointment of officers, must likewise share in their removal, Madison declared that the appointment of officers was a purely executive function. The Constitution placed the executive power in the President, making an exception in the power to appoint. It had made no exception in regard to removals. Exceptions from the separation of powers should be construed strictly to avoid destruction of the President's responsibility. Both houses of Congress agreed, and the laws creating government departments were worded so as to recognize the President's exclusive power to remove appointive officers.

Andrew Johnson thus had constitutional warrant for disregarding the Tenure of Office Act, but nearly a year went by with Secretary Stanton still in office. On January 30, 1868, an event occurred that revealed the Stevens faction's hair-trigger attitude toward impeachment and its sweeping concept of the power to impeach. Congressman Schofield of Pennsylvania took the floor in the House and read a short editorial from the Washington *Evening Express* of the previous day. The paper asserted that at a large social gathering one of the justices of the Supreme Court "declared in the most positive terms" that all the Reconstruction acts "were unconstitutional, and that the court would be sure to pronounce them so." Warned that such remarks were indiscreet, "he at once repeated his views in a more positive manner." The Baltimore *Gazette* named the speaker: Associate Justice Stephen J. Field, whom President Lincoln had appointed to office.

Schofield moved that the Judiciary Committee make an inquiry "and report whether the facts constituted such a misdemeanor in office as to require the House to present to the Senate articles of impeachment against the said justice of the Supreme Court." The motion was instantly approved, leaving no doubt that the Radical Republican majority regarded Justice Field's remarks as impeachable. Besides being an invasion of freedom of speech, the House action clearly meant that anything its members regarded as a "misdemeanor in office" was a constitutional ground of impeachment, even though it had not the faintest taint of criminality. Field's remark was an indiscretion, but no reasonable person could call it an impeachable misdemeanor. If the Constitution means what it says, both on impeachment and on attainder, nothing could more plainly stamp such an impeachment as a bill of attainder in disguise.

In three weeks, the impeachment move against Justice Field dropped out of sight and out of mind. For on February 21 President Johnson removed Secretary Stanton from office for undercutting Presidential policies. Three days later the House of Representatives, by a majority of 126 to 47, voted articles of impeachment against the President.

Eleven articles were presented, but ten related to the Stanton episode. Primarily, the House charged as a high crime and misdemeanor that on February 21 the President did unlawfully "issue an order in writing for the removal of Edwin M. Stanton from the office of Secretary for the Department of War . . . which order was unlawfully issued with intent then and there to violate the act entitled 'An act regulating the tenure of certain civil offices,' passed March 2, 1867."

In the only unrelated article, the House charged that Andrew Johnson did, on August 18, 1866, "deliver with a loud voice certain intemperate, inflammatory, and scandalous harangues, and did therein utter loud threats and bitter menaces as well against Congress as the laws of the United States duly enacted thereby." These were the impeachable words of the President, cited by the House Managers:

"We have witnessed in one Department of the Government every endeavor, as it were, to prevent the restoration of peace, harmony and union . . . we have seen Congress pretend to be for the Union when every step they took was to perpetuate dissolution, and make disruption permanent. We have seen every step that has been taken, instead of bringing about reconciliation and harmony, has been legislation that took the character of penalties, retaliation and revenge."

The citing of such sharp but orderly political remarks as a ground of impeachment stamped the movement for what it was—a determination to oust President Johnson because of hostility to his policies, not for any impeachable misconduct.

Notable among the seven House Managers were General Benjamin F. Butler of Massachusetts, a famous orator who was embroiled in controversy throughout his life; John A. Bingham of Ohio, leading drafter and congressional expositor of the Fourteenth Amendment; George S. Boutwell of Massachusetts, later Secretary of the Treasury under President Grant; and Thaddeus Stevens. They were armed with a brief on impeachment precedents furnished by Representative William Lawrence of Ohio.

President Johnson's quintet of legal defenders included some of the outstanding lawyers of the United States. Henry Stanbury resigned as Attorney General to head the group, but illness disabled him except for the opening and closing addresses to the Senate. Benjamin R. Curtis had been appointed to the Supreme Court in 1851 at the age of forty-one, but had resigned six years later in protest against the Dred Scott decision, from which he and one other justice dissented.* William M. Evarts, a recognized leader of the American bar for several decades, was also a diplomat without office: President Lincoln had sent him twice to

---

* Personal antagonism developed between Justice Curtis and Chief Justice Taney, who, after delivering the Court's opinion in *Scott*, rewrote it to cope with portions of the Curtis dissent.

England to dissuade the British government from aiding the Confederate navy. W. S. Groesbeck and Thomas A. R. Nelson completed the team.

The trial commenced in mid-March, three weeks after the impeachment, with General Butler opening for the Managers. He began adroitly by showing familiarity with and at the same time misrepresenting the famous trial of Warren Hastings in England:

"May it not have been that the trial then in progress [in 1787] was the determining cause why the framers of the Constitution left the description of offenses because of which the conduct of an officer might be inquired of to be defined by the laws and usages of Parliament as found in the precedents of the mother country, with which our fathers were as familiar as we are with our own?"

This question by its implications carried multiple distortions, both of the Hastings case itself and of the deductions to be drawn from it—distortions magnified by Hastings's acquittal. The seven-year Hastings trial was indeed cited by George Mason, but only as a reason for extending the grounds of impeachment beyond treason and bribery. Instead of supporting Butler's implication that the case carried impeachment beyond criminal misfeasance in office, the accusatory articles against Hastings piled crime on crime.

More subtle and even more misleading was Butler's equation of "high crimes and misdemeanors" with "the usages of Parliament as found in the precedents of the mother country." Those precedents included prosecutions forced on Parliament by omnipotent kings, prosecutions initiated by Parliaments snatching omnipotence away from the monarchs, and prosecutions that were mere outbursts of unreasoning passion. They reflected the violations more than the inclusions of the common law.

Later in the Johnson trial defense counsel Evarts exposed this perversion of history by showing that in the Hastings trial itself, British precedents on impeachment were repudiated. Lord Loughborough, said Evarts, sought "to demonstrate that the ordinary rules of proceeding in criminal cases did not apply to parliamentary impeachments, which could not be shackled by the forms observed in the Courts below" (that is, below the House of Lords). Evarts quoted the words by which Lord Thurlow overthrew this contention:

"My lords, with respect to the laws and usage of Parliament, I utterly disclaim all knowledge of such laws. It has no existence. True it is, in times of despotism and popular fury, when to impeach an individual was to crush him by the strong hand of power, of tumult, or of violence, the laws and usage of Parliament were quoted in order to justify the most iniquitous or atrocious acts. But in these days of light and constitutional government, I trust that no man will be tried except by the laws of the land, a system admirably calculated to protect innocence and to punish crime."

Thus whenever a representative or senator in Congress cites British precedent to justify going beyond the Constitution, he invokes "despotism and popular fury . . . the strong hand of power, of tumult, or of violence." Was that what the framers intended when they limited the grounds of impeachment to "high crimes and misdemeanors"?

General Butler, of course, ignored Lord Thurlow's denunciation of historic British practices that destroyed them as valid precedents. Instead, he sought to buttress his position by extended examples, contained in the brief submitted by Representative Lawrence, which he placed at this point in the record of the trial.

Lawrence cited case after case, from Hallam and other

legal historians, of great lords done to death by impeachment—and then undermined his cause by placing them in
Hallam's context of history, which supported Thurlow.
First employed by Edward III in 1376, the impeachment
process was set to one side by Tudor kings who found bills
of attainder more convenient. The House of Stuart brought
impeachment back. Between 1620 and 1688, it was employed forty times by Stuart kings or by a Parliament in
rebellion against those kings. Attainder and impeachment
as described by Hallam (as well as by historian Thomas
Erskine May) were used interchangeably to destroy political
offenders, and almost by the same process. Impeachment
permitted a defense before the House of Lords; attainder
had no standards.

It is impossible that the framers of our Constitution,
knowing this history, would have prohibited bills of attainder and yet allowed the same forbidden results, actuated
by the same passion, to be put into effect by a power of
impeachment modeled by silent implication on British
precedent. The debate in the Constitutional Convention,
the wording of the impeachment clauses, the wholehearted
devotion of the framers to liberty and justice, combine to
forbid such a thought. In portentous contrast, the spirit of
attainder ran through the trial of President Andrew Johnson. With truth, candor and impassioned rhetoric, Senator
Sumner revealed the political motive for the prosecution:

"Andrew Johnson is the impersonation of the tyrannical
Slave Power. In him it lives again . . . and he gathers about
him . . . partisans of slavery North and South. . . . With the
President at their head, they are now entrenched in the
Executive Mansion. Not to dislodge them is to leave the
country a prey to one of the most hateful tyrannies of
history."

It was in this manner that the entire prosecution of

President Johnson was conducted—in the spirit and actuality of a bill of attainder, with Johnson's counsel calling it by that name. It was brought in the form of impeachment solely because the Constitution prohibits bills of attainder. The House Managers thinly cloaked this purpose in their interpretations of the impeachment power.

General Butler put heavy reliance on Madison's remark in supporting the exclusive constitutional power of a President to remove his appointees from office, that if he made "wanton removal of meritorious officers," he would be subject to impeachment. Butler omitted the qualifying statement that the motive for such an action "must be that he may fill the place with an unworthy creature of his own." The Manager saw clear proof in this that the Senate had power to convict President Johnson for removing Secretary Stanton, regardless of the validity or invalidity of the Tenure of Office Act.

Such an argument revealed at one stroke the twin errors of Madison's statement and of the deduction Butler drew from it. In August 1867, without removing Stanton as Secretary of War, President Johnson nominated General Ulysses S. Grant to that position. The Senate, as was expected, defeated confirmation. The stage was set for Grant to seek the post by court action, thus testing the constitutionality of the Tenure of Office Act. However, the General refused to make the challenge. The Secretaryship of War was then offered to General William T. Sherman, who declined; political war was a bit too hellish. The President then removed Stanton and nominated Lieutenant General Lorenzo Thomas. None of these three men could be termed an "unworthy creature." Manager Bingham disclaimed criticism of Thomas; the crime was removal of Stanton. Thus by Madison's own terms, the President's removal of "meritorious" Secretary Stanton offered no constitutional ground of impeachment. Butler's misuse of Madison's words for such a purpose revealed the fallacy in Madison's argument, which he had thought up on the moment to score a point in polemics. General Butler summed up the Managers' position by quoting and concurring in these words of Representative Lawrence:

"We define therefore an impeachable high crime or misdemeanor to be one in its nature or consequences subversive of some fundamental or essential principle of government or highly prejudicial to the public interest, and this may consist of a violation of the Constitution, of law, of an official oath, or of duty, by an act committed or omitted, or, without violating a positive law, by the abuse of discretionary powers from improper motives, or for any improper purpose."

In other words, an impeachable misdemeanor was any action which the Senate regarded as improper, and which in its opinion proceeded from an improper motive. Butler turned to England for support:

"It is but common learning that in the English precedents the words 'high crimes and misdemeanors' are universally used; but any malversation in office highly prejudicial to the public interest, or subversive of some fundamental principle of government by which the safety of a people may be in danger, is a high crime against the nation, as the term is used in parliamentary law."

This obsolete British definition (done to death by Lord Thurlow) was the same as saying that President Johnson's 1866 speech criticizing Congress, and his transfer of the War Department from Edwin M. Stanton to Lorenzo Thomas, were impeachable either as "highly prejudicial to the nation" or as dangerous to the safety of its people. The Butler-Lawrence interpretation of "high crimes and misdemeanors" can be boiled down to the single word "maladministration," which the framers refused to put in the Constitution as a ground of impeachment. House Manager Bingham heightened this perversion of the framers' intentions by saying that in determining such grounds, the Senate was "a law unto itself"—a remark that gave the trial the precise quality of a bill of attainder.

Counsel for President Johnson referred to the 1789 debate in Congress on the President's power to remove officers, proving conclusively from Madison's speech (and acts of Congress based on it) that this power was recognized to lie in the President alone, unalterable by legislative action. General Butler conceded that if Johnson, instead of sending "his defiant message to the Senate," had said he was acting to test the constitutionality of the Tenure of Office Act, the House of Representatives might not have impeached him. So, said defense counsel Benjamin Curtis, the ground of impeachment was "not the removal of Mr. Stanton but the manner in which the President communicated the fact of that removal to the Senate after it was made."

Logically, this exchange of remarks, combined with the invalidity of the Tenure of Office Act, demolished the only charge against President Johnson that could fall within the definition of a "high misdemeanor." Curtis then proceeded to his main argument (which was a bit too broad, as it excluded all violations of state laws):

"My first position is, that when the Constitution speaks of 'treason, bribery, and other high crimes and misdemeanors,' it refers to, and includes, only high criminal offenses against the United States, made so by some law of the United States existing when the acts complained of were done, and I say that this is plainly to be inferred from each and every provision of the Constitution on the subject of impeachment."

He quoted the various clauses referring to "offenses,"

"conviction," "crimes," etc., in connection with impeachment, and said that the argument on this point was "vastly strengthened" by the Constitution's direct prohibition of bills of attainder and *ex post facto* laws. Curtis said:

"What is a bill of attainder? It is a case before the Parliament where the Parliament make the law for the facts they find. Each legislator (for it is in their legislative capacity they act, not in a judicial one) is, to use the phrase of the honorable Managers [Bingham], 'a law unto himself'; and according to his discretion, his views of what is politic or proper under the circumstances, he frames a law to meet the case and enacts it or votes in its enactment."

Still dwelling on Bingham's maladroit remark, Curtis went on:

"According to the doctrine now advanced bills of attainder are not prohibited by this Constitution; they are only slightly modified. It is only necessary for the House of Representatives by a majority to vote an impeachment and send up certain articles and have two thirds of this body vote in favor of conviction, and there is an attainder; and it is done by the same process and depends on identically the same principles as a bill of attainder in the English Parliament. The individual wills of the legislators, instead of the conscientious discharge of the duty of the judges, settle the result.

"I submit, then, Senators, that this view of the honorable Managers of the duties and powers of this body cannot be maintained."

In conclusion, Curtis turned to the article impeaching the President for slander of Congress in a speech. This, he said, was not only an attempt to set up an *ex post facto* law where none existed "prior to the act to punish the act"; it was a case where Congress was expressly prohibited, by the

First Amendment, from making any law whatever, even to punish subsequent speech.

What was this law on freedom of speech designed to be? Was it to be, "as the honorable Managers seem to think it should be, the sense of propriety of each Senator appealed to"? That was "the same freedom of speech, Senators, in consequence of which thousands of men went to the scaffold under the Tudors and the Stuarts. . . . Is that the freedom of speech intended to be secured by our Constitution?"

This trial, Curtis predicted, would live in history as the most conspicuous American example either of justice or of injustice. It would (to paraphrase Edmund Burke) either exemplify that justice which is the standing policy of all civilized states, or it would produce "that injustice which is sure to be discovered, and which makes even the wise man mad, and which, in the fixed and immutable order of God's providence, is certain to return to plague its inventors."

The House Managers continued to provide defense with openings to call the impeachment a bill of attainder. Later in the trial, defense counsel Groesbeck put some of these remarks together. Without naming the Managers, he said that one of them (it was Butler) had stated that in sitting as a court of impeachment, the Senate "knew no law, either statute or common, and consulted no precedents save those of parliamentary bodies." Another (it was Bingham) had claimed that the Senate "was a law unto itself; in a word, that its jurisdiction was without bounds; that it may impeach for any cause, and there is no appeal from its judgment." A third (John A. Logan) said much the same as Bingham.* And it was argued by Butler that when the

---

* Logan's words were: "Now, it is admitted by all sides that any officer may be removed under our laws for any reason, no reason, or for political

words "high crimes and misdemeanors" were used, "they are without signification and intended merely to give solemnity to the charge." Under these interpretations "everything this tribunal may deem impeachable becomes so at once." Said Groesbeck, pursuing the issue of attainder:

"To sustain this extraordinary view of the character of this tribunal we have been referred to English precedents, and especially to early English precedents, when, according to my recollection, impeachment and attainder and bills of pains and penalties labored together in the work of murder and confiscation."

The Constitution, Groesbeck declared, placed limitations on the executive and judicial departments, and he had supposed the legislative was also limited. But according to the argument made in this trial, it was otherwise. The Senate "has in its service and at its command an institution [impeachment] that is above all law and acknowledges no restraint; an institution worse than a court martial, in that it has a broader and more dangerous jurisdiction."

The question of attainder was sharpened by a vitriolic attack on Johnson by Thaddeus Stevens, who asserted that the Senate had rendered final judgment against Johnson even before the House impeached him. It did so, he declared, in a resolution adopted on February 21 (three days before the House acted) declaring that the President had no power to remove Stanton. By that vote, Stevens maintained, the senators were committed to find him guilty. Exclaimed the fiery Radical Republican leader:

---

reasons simply. . . . And as the phrase 'removal from office' is only found in the Constitution as the consequence of conviction upon impeachment . . . is it not equally certain that . . . an officer may be removed by impeachment for political reasons, as he may be for the same reasons by any department of the Government in which the right of removal is vested?" Logan's "reasoning," if it can be called that, strips the words "high crimes and misdemeanors" completely out of the Constitution.

"And now this offspring of assassination turns upon the Senate . . . and bids them defiance. How can he escape the just vengeance of the law? Wretched man, standing at bay, surrounded by a cordon of living men, each with the ax of an executioner uplifted for his just punishment!"

Defense counsel Evarts seized on this as one more proof that the Managers were seeking to pass a bill of attainder. If, said he, judgment was rendered in that vote of February 21, "then you are here standing about the scaffold of execution." If so, of what service was the constitutional prohibition of bills of attainder? He asked, as had a fellow counsel:

"What is a bill of attainder; what is a bill of pains and penalties? . . . It is a proceeding by the legislature as a legislature to enact crime, sentence, punishment all in one. . . . [If you follow the Stevens rule] you are enacting a bill of pains and penalties upon the simple form that a majority of the House and two thirds of the Senate must concur, and the Constitution and the wisdom of our ancestors all pass for naught."

To emphasize the element of attainder, Evarts quoted the admission of House Manager Buchanan in the case of Judge Peck that to convict the judge of impeachable official misbehavior, "we are bound to prove that the respondent has violated the Constitution or some known law of the land." He endorsed the argument of his colleague Curtis, "upon the strict constitutional necessity, under the clause prohibiting *ex post facto* laws, and under the clause prohibiting bills of attainder," that articles of impeachment be confined to "what is crime against the Constitution and crime against the law."

Here was the clearest statement that to go beyond crimes against the laws and Constitution and give sanction to general ideas of misbehavior was to convert impeachment into both a bill of attainder and an *ex post facto* law.* If the case of Warren Hastings was to be used as a guide, Evarts declared, the standard of impeachable misconduct must meet the specifications laid down by Edmund Burke as manager of the Hastings trial. He quoted Burke's opening address to the House of Lords:

"We know, as we are to be served by men, that the persons who serve us must be tried as men, and with a very large allowance indeed to human infirmity and human error. This, my lords, we knew, and we weighed before we came before you. But the crimes which we charge in these articles are not lapses, defects, errors of common human frailty, which, as we know, and feel, we can allow for. We charge this offender with no crimes that have not arisen from passions which it is criminal to harbor; with no offenses that have not their root in avarice, rapacity, pride, insolence, ferocity, treachery, cruelty, malignity of temper; in short, in nothing that does not argue a total extinction of all moral principle, that does not manifest an inveterate blackness, dyed ingrain with malice, vitiated, corrupted, gangrened to the very core."

Evarts could have carried his case further. For at the close of that seven years' trial the Lords, passing on Burke's catalog of heinous accusations, found Hastings not guilty.

---

* In *Calder* v. *Bull* (3 Dallas 385) Justice Samuel Chase treated bills of attainder and *ex post facto* laws as virtually synonymous, saying: "The prohibition against their making any *ex post facto* laws was introduced for greater caution, and very probably arose from the knowledge, that the parliament of Great Britain claimed and exercised a power to pass such laws, under the denomination of bills of attainder, or bills of pains and penalties." *Ex post facto* laws inflict punishment for acts which were not criminal when committed. Impeachment for noncriminal conduct does the same, and is to be classed as attainder because it is directed against a named individual.

They found that his conduct consisted, not of crimes in office, but of errors of judgment in performance of his duties as governor general of India. For these he could not properly be impeached. Thus prosecution and defense, in combination, narrowed the grounds of impeachment permissible under British precedents. Both sides cast aside the Tudor-Stuart concept of impeachment. The British reform went further: Public opinion in and out of Parliament discarded the entire institution of impeachment. Except for one trivial case a few years later, no impeachment has taken place in Great Britain from 1786 to the present. But members of Congress claim that the framers, without saying so, embodied British concepts of impeachment in the Constitution, and cite as their only evidence the fact that the Constitution was written during the Hastings impeachment—which put an end to the British system.

Evarts's quotation from Burke brought to a climax the fundamental defense of President Johnson: that the articles of impeachment brought against him constituted a bill of attainder. The argument was answered by total silence. Not once was the word "attainder" spoken by any House Manager, nor did any touch on the concept of attainder. Any attempt at rebuttal would have brought the issue fully before the Senate, and the weakness of the Managers' denials would have given their arguments a hollow ring. Even the admission that grounds of argument on attainder existed might have given a new aspect to the trial, producing in some senatorial minds an unwillingness to cast a vote for an unconstitutional conviction. Indeed, the one-sided discussion had that tendency, reducing the case against Johnson to two narrowly technical points—denial by the Managers that when the President removed Secretary Stanton, he intended to test the constitutionality of the Tenure of

Office Act, and the question of criminal libel in Johnson's criticism of Congress.

The defense met the first of these arguments by putting General William Tecumseh Sherman on the stand. He testified that when the post of Secretary of War was being offered to him, the President said: "If we can bring the case to the courts it would not stand half an hour." Pursuing that line, defense counsel Nelson argued that the Tenure of Office Act was unconstitutional, but that in any case impeachment was unwarranted because "the President acted from laudable and honest motives, and is not, therefor guilty of any crime or misdemeanor."

Manager Bingham brought the case against President Johnson to a close by defining freedom of speech in terms of the Sedition Act of 1798. This he linked with an 1806 set of Army regulations by Congress in which military officers and soldiers were made subject to court-martial for using "contemptuous or disrespectful words" against the President, Vice President, or Congress. If those two laws are constitutional, declared Bingham, seditious utterances "are indictable as misdemeanors, whether made by the President or anybody else, and especially in an official charged with the execution of the laws." Indeed, he continued, seditious utterances by an executive officer always were indictable at common law:

"But, say counsel, this is his guaranteed right under the Constitution. The freedom of speech, says the gentleman, is not to be restricted by a law of Congress. How is that answered by this act of 1806, which subjects every soldier in your Army and every officer in your Army to court-martial for using disrespectful words of the President or of the Congress or of his superior officers? The freedom of speech guarantied by the Constitution to all the people of the

United States, is that freedom of speech which respects, first, the right of the nation itself, which respects the supremacy of the nation's laws, and which finally respects the rights of every citizen of the Republic."

Thus an unconstitutional Sedition Act (so pronounced by the Supreme Court more than a century after it expired), and a military regulation laid down to maintain discipline in the Army, were to measure the right of the President of the United States to criticize Congress. What this meant was that the First Amendment was worthless without the enforcing strength of the Supreme Court. On the constitutional level, impeachment trials throughout American history have been prosecuted on the legal plane occupied by the Sedition Act of 1798. In every instance where the drive for impeachment has been politically motivated—the prosecutions of Judge Pickering, Justice Chase, and President Johnson, and the abortive moves against Justices Field and Douglas—the same passions that produced the Sedition Act of 1798 have inflamed and degraded the driving forces in Congress.

The ordeal of President Andrew Johnson ended on May 16, 1868, when, after a two-month trial, the Senate voted on the eleven articles of impeachment. The vote was the same on each: guilty, 35; not guilty, 19—only one short of the needed two thirds. Before the balloting began, Senator Lyman Trumbull of Illinois presented a written opinion in which he said:

"In view of the consequences likely to flow from this day's proceedings, should they result in conviction on what my judgment tells me are insufficient charges and proofs, I tremble for the future of my country."

The ferocity of the prosecution and closeness of the verdict combined to establish the Johnson impeachment as a menacing portent of the future. The failure of this case to serve as a permanent warning against perversion of the Constitution is more ominous still. Nevertheless, if the cogent and powerful arguments of the defense influenced a single senator—and they probably converted several—they prevented the deepest tragedy in American political history.

CHAPTER VIII

EVIL RESULTS

OF GOOD INTENTIONS

IN THE HUNDRED-ODD YEARS SINCE 1868, the House of Representatives has impeached one Secretary of War and five federal district judges. In all cases the intentions were good; in all the judicial cases, however, the grounds of impeachment were stretched beyond the necessities of the occasion and increasingly beyond the boundaries of the Constitution.

Two hours before the House voted to impeach Secretary of War William W. Belknap on April 4, 1876, he resigned and President Grant instantly accepted his resignation. The charges were that he had received $6,000 per year for several years for appointing one subordinate,* and $1,500 for each of seventeen other appointments. The payments were not disputed. Belknap's plea was that, as a private citizen, he was not liable to impeachment. The House Managers

---

*Post trader at Fort Sill in Indian Territory. A skeptical Senate heard the recipient testify that, grateful for this "lucrative" office, he began of his own free will and without solicitation to set up a trust fund for the education of the Belknaps' infant son.

held that he was liable because he resigned to escape impeachment; he countered that he did so to protect others whom he did not name. The trial turned into a debate among senators over jurisdiction, with special emphasis on the issue raised but not specifically decided in 1797: whether or not Congress, like the British Parliament, could use the impeachment process against non-officeholders.

Departing from custom, thirty senators turned in written opinions during the course of the trial, nearly all of them dealing with constitutional questions. Thus the trial produced a symposium of individual senatorial views on the scope of impeachment, rather than a judgment upon the guilt or innocence of the accused. Broadly, the question was whether the Constitution strictly defines the grounds of impeachment or allows varying degrees of latitude in that respect. The results were widely polarized, yet there was an extensive middle ground.

Senator Joseph E. McDonald of Indiana wrote that he had seen no case in early English history "which did not grow out of malconduct in office, or was not for some political offense, such as treason or the like." Senator William A. Wallace of Pennsylvania added that in the United States, impeachment had never been used or "understood to apply to the trial or punishment of citizens for personal crime as distinguished from official misconduct."

This viewpoint was challenged by Senator John J. Ingalls of Kansas, who said that an officeholder could be impeached and removed "for murder, arson, robbery, or any crime whose penalty is defined by law," and the offender was subject also to punishment in the courts.

Senator Frederick T. Frelinghuysen of New Jersey took a surprising stand against broad powers of impeachment that were drawn from early British practice. He had voted to convict President Johnson, but here, free of political motivation or Civil War emotions, he completely repudiated British practices and likened them to bills of attainder:

"The procedure of impeachment was imported into our Constitution from the common parliamentary law of England, but it was placed there clipped and pruned of very many of its baneful incidents. Impeachment, associated with bills of attainder and of pains and penalties and *ex post facto* laws, was made in Great Britain an instrument of political persecution and partisan aggrandizement. It was through those agencies that the grossest injustice was perpetrated in the name of law, that men of political power were destroyed, that families of influence were blotted out, and that their estates were confiscated to become a reward to those who persecuted those who owned them."

Senator William P. Whyte of Maryland disagreed with Frelinghuysen. Jurisdiction, he argued, was derived without limitation from the clauses saying that the House of Representatives shall have sole power to impeach and the Senate sole power to try impeachments. He reasoned:

"The makers of the Federal Constitution gave this power of trial by impeachment to the two Houses, as above stated, in all its plenitude, and then by subsequent special limitation restricted it in its details wherever they intended its power to be restrained [e.g., by limiting the punishment]. The power itself they never intended to curtail; for, when they added 'high crimes and misdemeanors' to treason and bribery, Col. Mason remarked: 'As bills of attainder, which have saved the British Constitution, are forbidden, it is the more necessary to extend the power of impeachment.' "

Whyte's apparent inference was that because bills of attainder were forbidden, Mason was suggesting that impeachment be given the scope of bills of attainder. But why forbid bills of attainder only to reestablish them under another name? Mason, addressing educated Americans of the eighteenth century, had had no need to spell out his position. He was merely saying that "treason and bribery" would not have caught the Earl of Strafford, whose execution under a bill of attainder notoriously "saved the British Constitution" from the absolutism of Charles I. Mason wanted to extend the grounds of action beyond the two crimes already specified, and he agreed with Madison that there must not be "tenure during the pleasure of the Senate." That would indeed make the process of removal synonymous with bills of attainder.

Furthermore, Mason's quoted remark refutes the argument of Senator Whyte (and many others during the past two centuries) that congressional jurisdiction is obtained, and made limitless, by the conferral in Article I of sole power on one house of Congress to impeach and on the other to try impeachments. If that were the case, Mason's motion would have nothing to do with the scope of an impeaching power made limitless by Article I. But his declared purpose was "to extend the power of impeachment." What need was there to extend the power if it already had been made plenary?

Senator Angus Cameron of Wisconsin refuted the argument of Senator Whyte and pointed out its implications:

"It follows, therefore, that if impeachment under our Constitution is as broad as impeachment under the English law, every citizen of the United States, whether he be a civil officer or a private person, can be impeached for any conduct which in the opinion of the two Houses of Congress is a high crime and misdemeanor. . . . I adopt the theory in regard to impeachment that in this country it is a proceeding established and limited by the Constitution, that it is not borrowed from the parliamentary law of England, but is a creation of the Constitution and consequently is strictly confined to the cases expressly enumerated in section 4 of article 2 of the Constitution."

Senator Charles W. Jones of Florida took a similar stand, observing that the argument for extended powers of impeachment (measuring the powers of Congress by English common law) were the same that had fastened on the country the "hated maxims" of the Alien and Sedition Acts. Said he:

"One of the most important, and at the same time the most dangerous features of this power is that it leaves to the two Houses of Congress an arbitrary discretion respecting the acts or conduct which shall subject officers to impeachment. No man knows, no man can know, what is an impeachable offense. . . . Under the law of impeachment as now understood how can any officer protect himself against those heats and passions of party which are inseparable from popular government if the doctrine of the managers shall prevail?"

Cameron thus reasserts that unlimited grounds of impeachment, employed under "the heats and passions of party," form the very essence of *ex post facto* laws and bills of attainder. Senators David McKay of Tennessee and Henry L. Dawes of Massachusetts sought to offset these arguments. One citing the case of a President, the other of a Chief Justice, they asked what would happen if such a man should become. imbecile by injury or disease and yet cling to office. He would not be guilty of treason, bribery, or any high crime or misdemeanor. How could he be removed, if not by impeachment?

To reach a case of this sort, both senators contended, the Constitution must be construed to permit impeachment for other causes than high crimes and misdemeanors. But if it were, House and Senate could impeach and remove for any

cause or for none at all, and the English system of the fourteenth century would return in all its barbarity. The answer
to the "imbecility" argument is that the price is too high
to pay for such poisonous preventive medicine. We would
be signing away basic liberties to cope with a disaster that
has never occurred (though there have been periods of
incapacity) since the impeachment clause came into effect
in 1789.

Senator Aaron H. Cragin of New Hampshire, remarking
that able senators had argued that the House of Representatives inherited all the impeachment powers of the House of
Commons, declared he could not subscribe to this doctrine:
"I do not believe that the bloody code of impeachment in
England was incorporated into our Constitution." He read
Madison's letter to Jefferson calling the universality of the
impeaching power "the most extravagant novelty that has
yet been broached," and concluded with these words:

"I place the opinion of James Madison against that of all
the Senators who believe in the universal power of impeachment."

Of twenty-four senators whose written opinions dealt with
the constitutional aspects of impeachment, sixteen took a
strict and limited view of permissible grounds. Eight took
a broader view, and of these three accepted the full range
of ancient British practice. The general rejection of the
broad view was striking when the Senate, on August 1, 1876,
held its final vote on the articles of impeachment. The
balloting produced 37 votes for Belknap's conviction and 25
for acquittal, 4 short of the two thirds necessary for removal from office. All but one of the senators who voted
for acquittal gave their reasons. Twenty-two said that the
Senate lacked jurisdiction over a civil officer who resigned
before he was impeached. Only two found Belknap "not
guilty on the facts" (one of these was from his home state of

Iowa). Two senators denied jurisdiction, yet voted to convict.

Considering the magnitude of the offense, the virtually unanimous conclusion that Belknap was guilty, and the tenor of the debate, the acquittal was a decided setback for the doctrine that the Constitution embodies the law and usage of the British Parliament on the subject of impeachment. Had this trend toward the strict interpretation continued, impeachment would not be a controversial issue today.

After Belknap's acquittal, twenty-seven years passed before another civil officer was impeached. Then within a space of thirty-three years came five impeachments of inferior-court federal judges. Two were acquitted, two convicted, and one escaped trial by resigning.

The cases were similar in two respects:

1. All involved conduct which, if knowingly and habitually engaged in, violated the judges' oath of office and could be fairly charged as "high misdemeanors."

2. All produced interpretations of the Constitution by well-disposed congressmen that went beyond the necessities of the case and threatened a reversion to the excesses of the Chase and Johnson impeachments.

The trial of U.S. Judge Charles Swayne of the district of Florida, impeached in 1903, tried in 1905, led to the first of these extravagant interpretations. It was more notable, however, for the refutation of them by his counsel. Swayne was charged with padding expense accounts, using property in receivership for his personal profit, and misusing contempt powers. He was acquitted on all counts, with no certainty whether this was for lack of proof, lack of gravity, or nonimpeachability on the charges.

Swayne's counsel made the most extended study of British precedents to be found in American impeachment annals.

They showed that the process was used from the Plantagenet through Stuart dynasties as a weapon against powerful political offenders, public and private, with an apparent limitation on its application to judges. Counsel John M. Thurston said:

"By the foregoing analysis of the only English precedents to which we can look for expositions of the meaning of the phrase 'high crimes and misdemeanors,' as applied to the conduct of English judges, the fact is put beyond all question that the only judicial acts which the House of Commons ever regarded as falling within that category are such acts as a judge performs while sitting upon the bench, administering the laws of the realm, either between private persons or between the Crown and the subject."

During the Stuart regime, Thurston observed, judges could be dismissed for no cause at all, at the will of the king. The 1701 Act of Settlement stabilized their position by giving them tenure "during good behavior," coupled with an additional liability—to removal by the king on the "address" to him of both houses of Parliament. Thurston gave the reason for this:

"But while the judges were being thus entrenched in their offices, the fact was not forgotten that the remedy by impeachment extended only to high crimes and misdemeanors which did not embrace personal misconduct. Therefore a method of removal was provided by address, which was intended to embrace all misconduct not included in the term 'high crimes and misdemeanors.' "

The framers of the Constitution, said Thurston, were fully aware of the nature and purposes of the two systems: to reach different types of conduct. With only one dissenting vote, they "rejected the proposition to embody the removal of Federal judges by address in the Constitution of the United States 'as weakening too much the independence of the judges.' " That left only impeachment for criminal misconduct as the method and grounds of removal.

For the prosecution, House Manager Henry W. Palmer of Pennsylvania went back to 1798 in arguing that jurisdiction in impeachments is derived from the conferral of "sole power" to impeach and to try, and that the clause on "high crimes and misdemeanors" is merely a requirement that persons convicted of such offenses be removed from office. There could be removal for other causes. In any event, he declared, the word "misdemeanor" is not strictly a criminal term but "covers every act of misbehavior in a popular sense." The framers, he contended, understood impeachment as it was then understood in England, where "any offense was impeachable that Parliament chose to so consider."

Swayne's acquittal did not stop the slide toward "tenure during the pleasure of the Senate" that had developed in the prosecution of this case. The subsequent impeachments of Judges Robert W. Archbald, George W. English, and Halsted L. Ritter furnished tempting openings for future congressmen to veer into partisan politics and pass bills of attainder under the guise of impeachment. Three decades later, these tendencies bore fruit in the attempt to impeach Justice Douglas.

The conduct of Judge Archbald was impeachable at worst, reprehensible in general. As a circuit judge of the Commerce Court, he used his position to induce railroads to sell or lease coal companies to him. He accepted $500 from one railroad for his support in litigation with another railroad over transfer of coal leases. He speculated in coal properties while on the court. He took money to intervene in cases before the Interstate Commerce Commission. In previous service as a district judge, he had "accepted loans" from lawyers and their clients while presiding over their cases. At his trial in 1913 Archbald admitted all the facts charged against him and merely denied criminal intent, although intent was implicit in the facts. The Senate removed him and disqualified him from holding office.

In a country club of financiers, nothing that Judge Archbald did would have subjected him to indictment or have set him completely apart from the other members. But in a judge, some of these actions were inherently criminal; they revealed a deliberate intent to violate his oath of office. The House Managers correctly made that charge but then went far beyond it, as did some of his judges in the Senate. Senator Elihu Root explained his vote in a well-grounded statement endorsed by Senator Henry Cabot Lodge. Root voted to convict Archbald "because I find that he used the power and influence of his office as judge of the Court of Commerce to secure favors of money value for himself and his friends from the railroad companies, some of which were litigants in his court. . . . I consider this course of conduct, and each instance of it, to be high crime and misdemeanor."

Indeed, who would adopt a different view? Senator Root emphasized his restricted position by saying that he had "voted 'not guilty' upon the other articles, because while most of them involve improper conduct, I do not consider that the acts proved are high crimes and misdemeanors." It was in the effort of the prosecutors to justify the other articles, and in the vote of the Senate upon them (guilty, 42; not guilty, 20; absent or not voting, 32) that the Archbald case departed profoundly from the constitutional grounds of impeachment. In their desperation, Archbald's own counsel made this departure easier by reverting to the extreme position that a misdemeanor must be indictable in order to be impeachable.

Manager John A. Sterling of Illinois went to the other extreme: The Constitution, he pointed out, "puts no limitation on the House of Representatives or the Senate on what constitutes these crimes, misdemeanors, and misbehaviors." No statutory or common law defined or limited them, he said. To find the limitations, one must go to the individual consciences of senators. He laid down this rule of guidance:

"And so, Mr. President, I say, that outside of the language of the Constitution, which I quoted there is no law which binds the Senate in this case today except that law which is prescribed by their own conscience, and on that, and on that alone, must depend the result of this trial. Each Senator must fix his own standard; and the result of this trial depends upon whether or not these offenses we have charged against Judge Archbald come within the law laid down by the conscience of each Senator for himself."

If that had been the intent of the framers, an appropriate wording of the Constitution would have been "Judges shall hold office during the pleasure of the Senate." House Manager George W. Norris of Nebraska (who had been elected to the Senate but had not yet transferred) arrived at a conclusion similar to Sterling's by another route—the "good behavior" clause. He said:

"If judges can hold their offices only during good behavior, then it necessarily and logically follows that they can not hold their offices when they have been convicted of any behavior that is not good. If good behavior is an essential of holding the office, then misbehavior is a sufficient reason for removal from office."

Congress has never had a member of higher character than Norris—honest, intelligent, liberal, and supremely devoted to the welfare of his country. But he assumed that the Senate as a body possessed his own excellencies, so that his high standards of morality and citizenship added to the ultimate evils resulting from his reasoning.

Of broader influence on congressional and legal thought than the opinions of Sterling and Norris was a widely read description of the Archbald case and earlier trials by Wrisley Brown. A special prosecutor in the Attorney General's office, Brown was loaned as counsel to the House Managers. Writing in the *Harvard Law Review* in 1913, he dismissed all impeachments that had resulted in acquittal as being "of little value as precedents because of their close intermixture of fact and law." This mingling, he said, made it practically impossible to determine whether the evidence was insufficient to support the charges, or whether the acts were insufficient to support impeachment. Thus he swept aside the Chase acquittal as a rebuke to those who use impeachment for political purposes. Noting, correctly, that Archbald's conduct could not have been punished if the judge had been a private citizen, Brown reached this peroration, technically sound but rhetorically misleading:

"Therefore, the judgment of the Senate in this case has forever removed from the domain of controversy the proposition that the judges are only impeachable for the commission of crime or misdemeanors against the laws of general application. The case is instructive, and it will go down in the annals of Congress as a great landmark of the law."

Certainly this remark is a talking point for those who wish to justify impeachment for any cause, no matter how far removed from the element of criminality. Brown's conclusion would have agreed with the facts, but the import would have been far different, if he had simply stated that the Senate held judges to be impeachable for gross and deliberate violations of their oath of office, as well as laws of general application.

Far more sweeping than Brown's opinion, however, was the judgment of William Howard Taft, addressing the American Bar Association a few months after he left the

White House in 1913. Said the former President and future Chief Justice of the United States, concerning the Archbald trial:

"By the liberal interpretation of the term 'high misdemeanor' which the Senate has given there is now no difficulty in securing the removal of a judge for any reason that shows him unfit."

Taft need not have used the last four words. Under the Archbald precedent, a judge could be removed for any reason. Taft's statement can with perfect logic be paraphrased to read: "By the interpretations given in the Archbald case, judges hold office during the pleasure of the Senate"—the exact situation which the framers tried to avoid by rewriting the impeachment clause. Under the Taft concept, who is to judge whether a judge is unfit? The Senate. What is the constitutional limit on charges? The sky. A better course could not be chosen for legalizing bills of attainder under the guise of impeachment.

Expansion of the Archbald decision, as thus interpreted, began in the next case—that of District Judge George W. English of East St. Louis, Illinois. English was impeached after the St. Louis *Post-Dispatch* exposed his administration of justice as an extortion racket. The accusations were so undeniably true and impeachable that the judge resigned before his trial could begin. The House, to prevent a useless interruption of congressional business, asked the Senate's consent to withdrawal of the impeachment. The Senate, though its loins were girded for battle, reluctantly agreed and the case was dropped.

All that came out of it was a new and enlarged definition of impeachability in the initiatory proceedings of the House of Representatives. But the enlargement was monumental; the House, after citing various valid grounds of action against public officers, produced this statement based on

Wrisley Brown's article and ex-President Taft's expansion of it:

"It is now, we believe, considered that impeachment is not confined alone to acts which are forbidden by the Constitution or federal statutes. The better sustained and modern view is that the provision for impeachment in the Constitution applies not only to high crimes and misdemeanors as those words were understood at common law but also acts which are not defined as criminal and made subject to indictment, and also to those which affect the public welfare. Thus an official may be impeached for offenses of a political nature and for gross betrayal of public interests."

By its very wording, this "modern view" destroys the constitutional prohibition of *ex post facto* laws. Who is to determine what conduct is politically improper, or what affects the public welfare sufficiently to warrant impeachment? The House and Senate, after the acts are performed. Grounding impeachment on such undefined criteria removes any possibility that the accused may know beforehand what he might be accused of. The law is written after the action is taken, which is the definition of *ex post facto*. Congressional enforcement of such a law against an individual is the essence of a bill of attainder. As defined by the Supreme Court in *Cummings* v. *Missouri*:

"A bill of attainder is a legislative act which inflicts punishment without a judicial trial."

Or as former Supreme Court Justice Curtis said in the impeachment trial of President Johnson:

"What is a bill of attainder? It is a case before the Parliament where the Parliament make the law for the facts they find. Each legislator . . . frames a law to meet the case and enacts it or votes in its enactment."

In the same case defense counsel Evarts stated:

"A bill of attainder . . . is a proceeding by the legislature as a legislature to enact crime, sentence, punishment all in one."

Do that, Evarts said, "and the wisdom of our ancestors all pass for naught." Yet the House of Representatives did do it in 1926, and worse was to come. In 1932 District Judge Harold Louderback was impeached on the charge of appointing incompetent receivers and allowing them excessive fees. In presenting the articles of impeachment, the House Managers not only disregarded the constitutional limitation to high crimes and misdemeanors but declared that it was not necessary to find the judge guilty of any misconduct. According to their report (italics added):

"From an examination of the whole history of impeachment and particularly as it relates to our system of government, when the facts proven with reference to a respondent are such as are reasonably calculated to arouse *a substantial doubt* in the minds of the people over whom that respondent exercises authority, that he is not brave, candid, honest, and true, there is no other alternative than to remove such a judge from the bench, because wherever doubt resides confidence cannot be present."

The Constitution contains no trace of such a power of removal; yet in the Louderback trial, even the defense counsel acquiesced in that construction. They obtained the judge's acquittal not by challenging the scope of the Senate's power, but by clearing their client of the weak charges against him. On the issue of authority, Louderback's counsel strategically yielded to the temper of the times. His lawyer joined the prosecution in giving judges tenure during the pleasure of the Senate:

"The Constitution of this country provides that an appointment of this kind is for life, depending on good behavior. So I have concluded, and I respectfully submit to you, that 'high crimes and misdemeanors' so far as this proceeding is concerned, means anything which is bad behavior, anything which is not good behavior."

The latest and in one respect most extraordinary of all impeachment trials was that of District Judge Halsted L. Ritter in 1936. The charges against him were impressive: promoting a lawsuit in his court and accepting $4,500 from a former law partner out of the fees Ritter allowed in the case (the crime of champerty); practicing law by continuing his partnership while serving as a federal judge, thereby receiving $7,500 from a real estate client; omitting this and other fees from his income tax returns.

Six of the articles of impeachment specified separate "high crimes and misdemeanors"; the seventh declared: "The reasonable and probable consequence of the actions or conduct of Halsted L. Ritter . . . is to bring his court into scandal and disrepute, to the prejudice of said court and public in the administration of justice therein, and to the prejudice of public respect for and confidence in the Federal judiciary, and to render him unfit to continue to serve as such judge." A summary of the six itemized charges followed, and the article concluded: "Wherefore the said Judge Halsted L. Ritter was and is guilty of high crimes and misdemeanors in office."

The Senate acquitted Ritter on six articles, falling one short of conviction on the first charge and a bit farther short on the next five. It then produced an exact two-thirds majority, 56 to 28, on the seventh catchall article. Thus after acquitting him of all six criminal charges individually, the Senate convicted Ritter of them collectively as proof of general unfitness. This action reduced the judgment to removal for bringing his court "into scandal and disrepute" —a test under which any judge could be removed for anything Congress disliked about his conduct. It extended an open invitation for political assaults on the legal or social philosophy of the Supreme Court. The strange outcome prompted a number of senators to give their reasons for voting as they did.

Four of them with impeccable liberal credentials—Borah, La Follette, Frazier, and Shipstead—issued a joint statement declaring that a judge may be removed for being "wanting in that 'good behavior' designated as a condition of his tenure of office by the Constitution although such acts as disclose his want of 'good behavior' may not amount to a crime." This, they believed, was in the minds of the framers when they drafted the "good behavior" provision of the Constitution: "As early as 1688 the good-behavior standard for the judiciary was adopted by the English Parliament,* nearly 100 years prior to the adoption of our Constitution, and as early as 1693 the English courts construed the meaning of good behavior in relation to its effect on the tenure of office of a judge."

Without identifying the case (a remarkable omission) the senators went on:

"In one of these decisions may be found the following language: 'It is an estate for life determinable upon misbehavior: for "during good behavior" is during life; it is so long as he doth behave himself well: i.e., if he behaves himself well in it so long as he lives he is to have it as long as he lives, during life and during good behavior.' "

This principle, the four senators stated, "was adopted by the framers of the Constitution"; hence the senators' conclusion that judges could be removed for ill behavior that did not amount to a crime.

---

* This was an error. Judicial tenure "during good behavior" was discussed in the 1688 debate on the Bill of Rights; it was passed a few years later but rejected by William III, and was finally incorporated in the 1701 Act of Settlement.

Running down the tabulation of subjects in *Comyn's Digest of the Laws of England,* one comes to the title *Custos Rotulorum,* which would cover the statute of Henry VIII on "good behavior" of the clerk of the peace (already discussed in Chapter IV). Conspicuous among the citations under it is "1 Sho. 506," which turns out to be Shower's report of *Harcourt* against *Fox,* decided in the Court of King's Bench in 1693. It is the case in question.

Instead of involving the removal of a judge by his fellow judges for departure from "good behavior" (as one would deduce from the senators' statement), it was an "action on the case" by Simon Harcourt to recover fifteen shillings from John Fox. Actually, however, Harcourt was seeking to recover the position of clerk of the peace, from which he had been fired in spite of tenure "during good behavior." His behavior was not in question. The *custos* who appointed him (the Earl of Clare) had been removed by King William III. The new *custos,* the Lord of Bedford, discharged Harcourt and appointed Fox. At issue was the 1689 revision of the act of Henry VIII, by which the power to remove the clerk of the peace was transferred from the *custos* to the justices of the peace. Did the clerk have life tenure, subject to good behavior, or could each *custos* name his own clerk?

Harcourt was represented by one of the most prominent lawyers in England, Serjeant-at-Law Sir Cresswell Levintz. The Serjeant opened by telling Lord Chief Justice Holt and his associates that he had suffered a personal experience with a direct bearing on this case. He did not explain it; there was no need to. Promoted by James II from Attorney General to Justice of the King's Bench, he had been ousted from office after telling the king (who had asked his advice) that the monarch could not lawfully do what he wanted to do.

Levintz won the case, both in the King's Bench and in an appeal to Parliament. In this appeal Levintz used the language which the four senators attributed to the judges in their unidentified case. Thus instead of being spoken by English judges removing a colleague for misbehavior, the words were those of the foremost British defender of judicial independence—himself a victim of the very procedure the senators construed his words to defend. His intention was not to sanction easy removal from office, but to restore a "good behavior" appointee who had been improperly removed. When the sentence quoted by the four senators is reexamined, it becomes clear that not a single word supports the construction they put on it. Everything in the case points to the contrary—that removal for a lapse from good behavior must be for criminal misconduct. Said Serjeant Levintz, concerning the clerk's office held during good behavior:

"I say it is no hurt to anybody that it should be an office for life, for it has an annexed condition to be forfeited *upon misdemeanor.*"

The senators could have found similar statements made by the judges in that case. Concerning the original statute of Henry VIII, Justice Sir Giles Eyres said: "The words, 'unless displaced by the *custos*,' I take it, are to be interpreted *for misdemeanor.*"

Regarding the change in the method of removing the clerk, Justice Sir William Gregory declared: "Whereas before he was removable *for misdemeanor* by the *custos*, now that power is transferred to the justice of the peace at their quarter sessions."

Lord Chief Justice Holt made it unanimous that any removal must be for misdemeanor. Concerning the alteration in removal of the clerk and the grounds of removal, he said: "For before this act the justices of the peace could not remove him *for misdemeanor,* but the *custos* was to do it, because he put him in."

Thus Chief Justice Holt, his two associate justices, and the winning lawyer, whose words were perverted by the senators, all used the term "misdemeanor"—connoting criminality—as the ground of removal for lapse from "good behavior." No wonder the four senators decided not to identify the case from which they quoted. Having reached their conclusion, based on distortion of this unidentified English case, that judges could be removed for acts which "may not amount to a crime," Borah and his colleagues proceeded to turn it into a positive provision of the Constitution:

"Our federal judges are appointed for life, conditioned upon their good behavior, and if they fail in this respect they may be impeached and removed from office. This, we feel, is a wise provision of the Constitution, and that its enforcement is necessary in order to maintain respect for and the integrity of our courts."

Not only is such a "provision of the Constitution" nonexistent, but the inferences drawn to support it are directly contradicted by the action of the framers on August 27, 1787, when they considered and defeated a motion that would have embedded a removal provision in the appointment clause. After they voted that judges "shall hold their offices during good behavior," a motion was made to add a provision for their removal by joint action of the President, Senate, and House. As described in Chapter 1, it was assailed on all sides as "arbitrary," "dangerous," and "weakening too much the independence of the judges." The motion was voted down, seven states to one. This left the removal of judges strictly limited to impeachment for and conviction of "high crimes and misdemeanors." Tenure "during good behavior" could be terminated only by that process and only on those grounds.

The verdict in the Ritter case was vigorously protested by Senator Warren Austin of Vermont. "The sum of six acquittals," he said, "cannot be a conviction." Article 7, he pointed out, made no charge of evil intent, corruption, or illegality. Six previous votes had acquitted Ritter of such charges. "The necessary conclusion is that a Federal judge has been removed from his office for general misbehavior not amounting to a crime."

Reciting five provisions of the Constitution in which impeachment was equated with criminal offenses and proceedings, he said this was the first time in history in which the words "have been interpreted to connote general misbehavior" without a two-thirds finding of "evil intent, corruption or illegality." In reply to the argument that impeachment was not a criminal proceeding, but a mere inquiry into fitness for office, he quoted Justice Joseph Story's *Commentaries on the Constitution:*

"It is the boast of English jurisprudence—and without it the power of impeachment would be an intolerable grievance—that in trials by impeachment the law differs not in essentials from criminal prosecutions before inferior courts. The same rules of evidence, the same legal notions of crimes, and punishments prevail."

Austin concluded that without the element of "evil intent, corruption, or illegality," Judge Ritter was innocent both of "general misbehavior" and of "high crimes and misdemeanors."

Senator Hiram Johnson of California challenged those who convicted Ritter to produce any case of impeachment, either of a judge or of an inferior official, in federal or state trials, "where an acquittal of all the charges separately was transmitted into a shotgun decision of guilty upon some of them collectively." "Of course," he said, "it would be presumptuous for any humble member of the Impeachment Court to disagree with the new profound constitutional expounders of the Senate" who had found the judge guilty "under the generic and mystic term of 'misbehavior.'" In the same ironic vein he exposed the deeper significance of their action:

"I would not be so bold as dogmatically to insist that the great constitutional expounders of the Senate wholly erred in their construction of the Constitution; but the proposition that the discretion vested in the Senate in impeachment proceedings is absolute and unrestrained I cannot for an instant subscribe to."

Remarking on the similarity of "misbehavior" to "maladministration," Senator Johnson quoted the debate in the Federal Convention on the latter word as a ground of impeachment, and described its rejection after Madison's protest that it would "be equivalent to a tenure during the pleasure of the Senate." From this it appears, he said, "that the very vague and indefinite term so beloved by impeachers was apparently in the minds of the framers of the Constitution when that document was written, and the idea of the tenure of judges at the pleasure of the Senate, so ably argued by some today, was rejected by our forefathers."

Indeed, it was to guard against politics, passion, and arbitrary use of power that the framers overwhelmingly defeated a motion to make judges removable for absence of "good behavior." It was to avoid abuses from these causes that they refused to make maladministration a ground of impeachment. But "maladministration" is a perfect synonym for the concept of impeachment that has been inching up on us for nearly a hundred years in House impeachments and Senate trials. Germinating in an almost invisible crack in the limitation against abuse of impeachment (that is, the small opening created by the absence of a definition of "high crimes and misdemeanors"), this false growth threatens to split the rock of the Constitution.

CHAPTER IX

THE REMEDY

IN THE DREAM WORLD of Senators Borah, La Follette, Frazier, and Shipstead, high-minded senators were to exercise a benevolent protectorate over the judiciary by removing judges for anything that tended to bring the judiciary into disrepute. On April 15, 1970, Minority Leader Gerald Ford transmuted their words into the reality of partisan politics with an accurate paraphrase of their dictum:

"What, then, is an impeachable offense? The only honest answer is that an impeachable offense is whatever a majority of the House of Representatives considers it to be at a given moment in history; conviction results from whatever offense or offenses two-thirds of the other body considers to be sufficiently serious to require the removal of the accused from office."

In short, by a sequence of four stretching operations between 1912 and 1936, the words "high crimes and misdemeanors"—the only constitutional grounds of removal from office—had been converted into the system James Madison said they were designed to prevent: "tenure during the pleasure of the Senate." Ford's sinister statement was fittingly embedded in his charges against Douglas, in which falsehoods and insinuations were employed to create that "sense of scandal" in the public mind whose mere existence, with or without just cause, was regarded by the Borah group as constitutional warrant for impeachment and removal.

Chairman Celler and his associates on the Judiciary subcommittee reviewed the clauses of the Constitution bearing on impeachment. Judges, they concluded, could be removed only through impeachment, and "for a judge to be impeached, it must be shown that he has committed treason, accepted a bribe, or has committed a high crime or misdemeanor." This conclusion may seem commonplace, since it is exactly what the Constitution says, but for a committee of Congress to accept it is unusual. It knocks out the arguments of House Managers in every impeachment trial of the twentieth century. Managers have contended, and the Senate in the Ritter case decided, that a judge can be removed for anything regarded as "misbehavior," with "high crimes and misdemeanors" attached as mere words without criminal import.

The subcommittee recognized that "Constitutional safeguards to assure a free and independent judiciary make it difficult to remove a Federal judge who may be unfit, whether through incompetence, insanity, senility, alcoholism, or corruption." On that score they quoted Alexander Hamilton in *The Federalist* (No. 79): "The want of a provision for removing the judges on account of inability has been a subject of common complaint. But all considerate men will be sensible that such a provision would either not be practiced upon or would be more liable to abuse than calculated to answer any good purpose."

Turning to the impact of judicial tenure "during good behavior," the subcommittee said: "All conduct that can be impeached must be at least a 'misdemeanor.' . . . Conduct which fails to meet the standard of 'good behavior,' but which does not come within the definition of 'misdemeanor' is not subject to impeachment." The subcommittee then took up the meaning of misdemeanor, quoting the opposing views of attorney Bethel Kelley for Representative Ford and Judge Simon H. Rifkind for Justice Douglas.

As Kelley saw it, "Congress has the power and duty to remove from office any judge whose proven conduct, either in the administration of justice or in his personal behavior, casts doubt on his personal integrity and thereby on the integrity of the entire judiciary." Rifkind asserted that the early history of high crimes and misdemeanors "reinforces their plain meaning." Even when the Jeffersonians "attempted to purge the federal bench of all Federalist judges," they felt compelled to charge high misdemeanors. "The unsuccessful attempt to remove Justice Chase firmly established the proposition that impeachment is for *criminal* offenses only, and is not a 'general inquest' into the behavior of judges." No judge had ever been removed except for criminal offenses.

The subcommittee presented two concepts of impeachment, which may be called the Celler concept and the Ford concept. Comparing them, the subcommittee found them alike in relation to behavior connected with judicial office or exercise of judicial power. Under both concepts relating to official actions, judges could be impeached for:

1. "Criminal conduct.
2. "Serious dereliction from public duty."

The great difference lay in "behavior not connected with the duties and responsibilities of the judicial office." Here, the subcommittee concluded, Celler's concept sanctioned removal only for criminal conduct. Ford's concept permitted removal either for criminal conduct or "serious dereliction from public duty."

The distinction between judicial and nonjudicial activities is logical. Serious (therefore deliberate) dereliction from public duty, in relation to the duties and responsibilities of office, would be a violation of the oath of office—a criminal offense and easily provable, though not a basis for prosecution in the courts. But what is "serious dereliction from public duty" unconnected with office, as presented in Ford's concept? It is anything that can be conjured up, imagined, or falsely charged, or anything that conflicts with prevailing ideas of decorum. A justice could be impeached for shaving his scalp or not cutting his hair—or, as Senator Hiram Johnson said in his bitter dissent in the Ritter case, for "sipping a cocktail before dinner" in Prohibition days.

The subcommittee's vindication of Douglas was so complete that it put an end to the ill-starred impeachment campaign. Celler and his subcommittee associates, after adopting their "return to the Constitution" concept of impeachment, did not submit the two concepts to the full committee. To have done so might have stretched out the proceedings interminably. Instead, they placed it before Congress and the country for thought and future influence. But there is no assurance that this "new" concept (actually as old as the trial of Justice Chase) will be adhered to. And it is not foolproof. For whenever the two houses have the determination and the votes to get rid of a judge for reasons of party or prejudice, anything they may choose to regard as a violation of the oath of office becomes so by their decree.

This brings us back to the basic defense in the impeachment of President Andrew Johnson—that impeachment without constitutional warrant is a bill of attainder. Such impeachment is also an *ex post facto* law. The Constitution says: "No bill of attainder or *ex post facto* law shall be passed." Once these constitutional realities are recognized in relation to impeachment, the entire situation falls into focus and the remedy is at hand.

Bills of attainder under any guise are subject to judicial review, and so are *ex post facto* laws. Thus judicial review constitutes the only protection against these prohibited actions by Congress. That is the basic provision of the Constitution for protection against legislative tyranny. Judicial review of bills of attainder was affirmed by way of illustration in *Marbury* v. *Madison* in 1803. It has been universally recognized by Congress. It was tacitly recognized but not acknowledged by the impeachers of Andrew Johnson, in their studious avoidance of the issue of attainder raised by defense attorneys Curtis, Evarts, and Groesbeck.

Following the injection of that issue into the Johnson trial by former Supreme Court Justice Curtis, Manager John Bingham, without saying a word about attainder, launched a violent attack against the idea of review of impeachment by the Supreme Court. It was a subject about which defense counsel had not uttered a syllable, but Bingham recognized that if the attainder label stuck, conviction of the President would be appealable to the Supreme Court. He said:

"The question which the gentlemen raise here in argument now is, in substance and in fact, whether . . . they cannot at last strip the people of the power which they retained to themselves by impeachment—to hold such malefactors to answer before the Senate of the United States, to the exclusion of the interposition of every other tribunal of justice upon God's footstool. What has this question to do with the final decision of the case before the Senate? I say if your Supreme Court sat today in judgment upon this question it has no power and can have none over the Senate. The question belongs to the Senate, in the language of the Constitution, exclusively. The words are that 'the Senate shall have the sole power to try all impeachments'!"

This, Bingham declared, covered every aspect of the case:

"The sole or only power to try impeachments includes the power to try and determine every question of law and fact arising in a case of impeachment. It is in vain that the decision of the Supreme Court or of the circuit court or of the district court or of any court outside of this [the Senate] is invoked for the decision of any question arising in this trial, between the people and their guilty President."

Had the clause relating to the Senate's "sole power" stood alone, there would be some slight plausibility to Bingham's interpretation. But the true meaning is found in its relation to a preceding clause. Putting the two together:

"The House of Representatives . . . shall have the sole power of impeachment.

"The Senate shall have the sole power to try all impeachments."

In combination, what are these but a mere division of functions between House and Senate? They say that the Senate shall have no part of the power to impeach, and that the House shall have no part of the power to try impeachments.

This was recognized in 1805 in the trial of Justice Chase. Combating the claim of the House Managers that "the sole power of impeachment" embraced power to impeach for any cause, defense counsel Joseph Hopkinson replied that the clause was intended "merely to declare in what branch of the Government it shall commence." The whole system of impeachment, Hopkinson declared, "must be taken together, and not in detached parts; and if we find one part of the Constitution declaring who shall commence an impeachment, we find other parts declaring who shall try it, and what acts and what persons are Constitutional subjects of this mode of trial."

In the Johnson case, after defense counsel Evarts and Groesbeck resumed the attainder theme opened by Curtis, Manager Bingham renewed his assault on Supreme Court jurisdiction. Again he avoided the fatal phrase "bill of attainder." He said:

"The Senate, having the sole power to try impeachments, must of necessity be vested by every intendment of the Constitution with the sole and exclusive power to decide every question of law and of fact involved in the issue . . . and the Supreme Court of the United States has no more power to intervene either before or after judgment in the premises than does the Court of St. Petersburg; and so the people of the United States, I hesitate not to say, will hold."

He backed this with another impediment to judicial review. Quoting the provision of Article III that "The judicial power shall extend to all cases in law and equity arising under this Constitution, the laws of the United States, and treaties made, or which shall be made," he protested:

"Impeachment is not a case 'in law or equity,' within the meaning of the terms as employed in the third section of the Constitution, which I have just read. It is in no sense a case within the general judicial power of the United States."

This expanded Bingham's original fallacy that the Senate's "sole power to try all impeachments" (a mere denial to the House of any share in the trial) gives the Senate power to override constitutional limitations without judicial review. If impeachment, by its very nature, cannot produce a "case in law or equity" when conducted in violation of the Constitution, that rule must apply to state as well as federal impeachments. It would follow, then, that states could set up racial qualifications and remove Negro officers by impeachment (there have been times when this could have happened), with no possibility of appeal to the Supreme Court under the Fourteenth Amendment. Confining the matter to the federal arena, the Senate could ignore the command that when sitting as a court of impeachment its members "shall be on oath or affirmation." Or House and Senate, acting together, could extend liability to include the impeachment of private citizens and their perpetual disqualification to hold office. Under Bingham's construction, such violations of the Constitution would not produce a case in law or equity for the victims of them.

Every unconstitutional action of Congress that works definite and substantial injury to a specific individual gives that person standing to present a "case in law or equity" to the courts of the United States. The only question, therefore, is whether removal by impeachment in violation of the Constitution produces substantial injury. Financially it may be no injury at all, but in social standing and human dignity the penalty is fearful. Suppose, however, that we treat it as only a passing episode of little stigma. What about the provision that the party convicted may be disqualified "to hold any office of honor, trust or profit under the United States"? Nobody, surely, would contend that this lifelong punishment, if imposed in violation of the Constitution, is too trivial to give rise to a case in law or equity. But no distinction based on differing penalties can be drawn. If a case in law or equity exists in relation to perpetual disqualification, it must exist in relation to every violation of constitutional provisions on impeachment.

Above all, this right of judicial review is implicit in the

prohibition of bills of attainder and *ex post facto* laws—the only processes of criminal law that are singled out by the original Constitution (there are others in the amendments) for complete and unqualified prohibition of action by Congress.* Thus they stand out above all others within the mandate that the judicial power shall extend "to all cases in law or equity" arising under the Constitution.

When the Johnson defense counsel injected the issue of attainder into the trial, they had no thought of seeking a review by the Supreme Court in case of conviction. They were well aware of what would result: A House and Senate having the votes and the will to remove the President would, by converting impeachment into attainder, do the same to the Supreme Court. Every justice who voted to reverse the conviction could himself, in defiance of the Constitution, be impeached and removed from office.

Curtis, Evarts, and Groesbeck were bent on saving the President, not on establishing a principle for future guidance. Accordingly they kept still about judicial review as a concomitant of attainder, just as the House Managers did about attainder itself. Indeed, former Justice Curtis accepted the political fact of the nonexistence of review and sought to turn Bingham's argument against the Managers. The absence of review, he said, imposed an additional duty upon the Senate to accept for itself, and be governed by, the principles of judicial review. The Senate, he observed, had excluded "the whole range of evidence relating to the public character" of President Johnson and the difficulties of his current task. That exclusion ought to be reversed. Said Curtis:

---

*Almost complete protection is afforded by the provision that "The privilege of the writ of *habeas corpus* shall not be suspended, unless when in cases of rebellion or invasion the public safety may require it."

"When a court [the Senate] sits only for a special trial, when its proceedings are incapable of review, when neither its law nor its fact can be dissected, even by reconsideration within its own tribunal, the necessary consequence is that when you come to make up your judgment, either you must take as for granted all that we offered to prove . . . or else it is your duty . . . to resume the trial and call in the rejected evidence. I submit it to you that a court without review, without a new trial, without exception [to rulings], and without possible correction of errors, must deal with evidence in this spirit and upon this rule."

Thus both sides excluded judicial review as a practicality in the case of Andrew Johnson, but both saw it looming in the background of the attainder issue. The House Managers, of course, regarded it as a menace, while Curtis attempted to install the principles of judicial review into the minds of the senators.

The message is clear: If the Supreme Court has no power to draw a line between constitutional impeachment and unconstitutional bills of attainder, the way is open to subject the judiciary to legislative control. Not only that, but the entire electoral process can be subverted.

Imagine a situation in which a totalitarian-minded President grooms a like-minded Cabinet officer as his successor, and is confronted with an overwhelmingly adverse Congress. Alarmed at the prospect of subversion of government, the House impeaches the Cabinet member for publishing a fascistic or communistic book. The Senate convicts him and bars him in perpetuity from holding "any office of honor, trust, or profit." That would be a bill of attainder, unmistakably stamped as such in purpose and effect, and yet might be designed by honorable men to "save the Constitution." Would the Supreme Court have no power to review it as a bill of attainder? If the Court refused to assert jurisdiction on that issue, the Constitution would not be saved; it would be destroyed, either by Presidential seizure of power or by the establishment of a legislative dictatorship.

Alexander Hamilton recognized the fundamental role of an independent judiciary. He focused on its power to invalidate bills of attainder when he wrote in *The Federalist* (No. 78):

"The complete independence of the courts of justice is peculiarly essential in a limited Constitution. By a limited Constitution, I understand one which contains certain specified exceptions to the legislative authority; such for instance, as that it shall pass no bills of attainder, no *ex post facto* laws, and the like. Limitations of this kind can be preserved in practice no other way than through the medium of courts of justice, whose duty it must be to declare all acts contrary to the manifest tenor of the Constitution void. Without this, all the reservations of particular rights or privileges would amount to nothing."

Hamilton's argument, which contains the genesis of *Marbury* v. *Madison,* is enough in itself to bring "attainder by impeachment" within the scope of judicial review. Combating the specious claim then in circulation that judicial review of acts of Congress "would imply a superiority of the judiciary to the legislative power," Hamilton enlarged on his theme:

"There is no position which depends on clearer principles, than that every act of a delegated authority, contrary to the tenor of the commission under which it is exercised, is void. No legislative act, therefore, contrary to the Constitution, can be valid. To deny this, would be to affirm, that the deputy is greater than his principal; that the servant is above his master; that the representatives of the people are superior to the people themselves; that men acting by virtue of powers, may do not only what their powers do not authorize, but what they forbid."

Exemption from that rule, Hamilton declared, could occur only through specific exceptions written into the Constitution:

"If it be said that the legislative body are themselves the constitutional judges of their own powers, and that the construction they put upon them is conclusive upon the other departments, it may be answered, that this cannot be the natural presumption, where it is not to be collected from any particular provisions in the Constitution."

The House Managers of Andrew Johnson's trial first affirmed the existence of inherent general powers in the Senate, then resorted to exceptions from the exceptions stated by Hamilton, without saying what those exceptions were. (As always, they were afraid to utter the phrase "bills of attainder.") After declaring that the Senate was restrained by "no law, either statutory or common," that it "was a law unto itself," that "it may impeach for any cause"—all of which appeared to impute senatorial omnipotence by divine right—the Managers turned to a specific exception from Hamilton's list of exceptions from legislative power. This exception was the Senate's "*sole power* to try all impeachments," which, according to the Managers, exempted impeachment from the prohibition of attainder. But that clause, as has been shown, was a mere denial of any part of the trial power to the House of Representatives.

Shall such illogic be permitted to expand impeachment to illimitable proportions in defiance of the express provisions of the Constitution, and at the same time to nullify the express prohibition of bills of attainder and *ex post facto* laws? Shall such prohibited laws be permitted against the President, Vice President, and all civil officers of the United States, on the pretense that the prohibitions of the Constitution are overridden by the single word "sole," which was designed only to separate the functions of House and Senate in the impeachment process? To achieve that, *Marbury* v. *Madison* would have to be overridden by Congress and abandoned by the descendants of John Marshall on the Supreme Court.

There is nothing in the Constitution, some may say, that empowers the Supreme Court to forestall or override an impeachment conviction, even though it clearly violates the Constitution. But there is also nothing in the Constitution that empowers the Supreme Court to override any act of Congress on any subject, for any reason. The power to do so came into force in 1803 in *Marbury* v. *Madison,* as the only means (and the intended means) of preserving the Constitution against intentional or unconscious deviations from it by acts of Congress.

In the opinion supporting that decision, Chief Justice Marshall followed the reasoning of Alexander Hamilton in *The Federalist.* And like Hamilton, in illustrating the imperative necessity of such a power, he emphasized the clause prohibiting bills of attainder and *ex post facto* laws. Challenging those who contended that when a law conflicts with the Constitution, "the courts must close their eyes to the Constitution, and see only the law," Marshall wrote:

"This doctrine would subvert the very foundation of all written constitutions. It would declare that an act which, according to the principles and theory of our government is entirely void, is yet, in practice, completely obligatory. . . .

"The constitution declares 'that no bill of attainder or *ex post facto* law shall be passed.' If, however, such a bill should be passed, and a person should be prosecuted under it; must the court condemn to death those victims whom the constitution endeavors to preserve?"

The subjection of bills of attainder to judicial review makes it abundantly evident that the power of review is not limited to laws of general application. A bill of attainder by its very nature applies only to specific individuals— either to one or more named persons, or to identifiable groups or classes. Impeachment affects only one named person, and that person's constitutional rights are not reduced by his employment as a civil officer of the United States.

Attainder is attainder under any guise. This principle was asserted at the very outset of government under the Constitution and was affirmed by the Supreme Court in the first cases arising under the attainder clause. In 1794 Federalist partisans in Congress sought to make political capital out of the Whisky Rebellion by falsely placing responsibility on the newly organized Democratic Societies, the grass-roots element in Jeffersonian Democracy. Without being named, the societies were made the subject of the following resolution introduced in the House:

"As part of this subject, we cannot withhold our reprobation of the self-created societies, which have risen up in some parts of the Union, misrepresenting the conduct of the government, and disturbing the operations of the laws, and which, by deceiving and inflaming the ignorant and the weak, may naturally be supposed to have stimulated and urged the insurrection."

The charge was contrary to fact, but its falsity was not the basis of the protests that arose in the House. "Opinions," declared James Madison, "are not the objects of legislation." The resolution, he said, threatened to impinge on freedom of speech and the press; moreover, to direct it against individuals violated an express provision of the Constitution:

"It is in vain to say that this indiscriminate censure is no punishment. If it falls on classes, or individuals, it will be a severe punishment. [I wish] it to be considered how extremely guarded the Constitution was in respect to cases not within its limits. . . . Is not this proposition, if voted, a vote of attainder?"

Legislatively, a *vote* of attainder is not a *bill* of attainder, but that distinction was immaterial. "If it be admitted," said Madison, "that *the law* cannot animadvert on a particular case, neither can we [the House] do it." The resolution was defeated.

The bills of attainder which the Supreme Court struck down in 1868 were not labeled as such. One required a loyalty oath by clergymen, the other by lawyers, as a prerequisite to practicing their professions. The Court went beyond the name to the essence and declared both to be bills of attainder. On February 1, 1943, Martin Dies of the House Committee on Un-American Activities denounced three named federal officers as "irresponsible, unrepresentative, crackpot, radical bureaucrats." At his instigation Congress placed a "rider" on an appropriation bill forbidding the payment of their salaries. The Supreme Court unanimously condemned this action, holding that its "effect was to inflict punishment without the safeguards of a judicial trial," and that in consequence it was a bill of attainder.

Dissenting from a decision upholding the conviction of Lloyd Barenblatt for contempt of Congress, Justices Black, Warren, Douglas, and Brennan put the stamp of attainder on the House Un-American Activities Committee itself. That committee, wrote Justice Black, had informed Congress in so many words that its "real purpose" in examining this man was to protect constitutional democracy "by turn-

ing the light of pitiless publicity" on those whom they regarded as subverters of it. "Such publicity," wrote Black,
"is clearly punishment, and the Constitution allows only
one way in which people can be convicted and punished . . .
by court and jury after a trial with all judicial safeguards."

A striking analogy exists between the claimed exemption
of House and Senate from judicial review of impeachment
proceedings that violate the Constitution, and the same
immunity which was once claimed with respect to cases of
contempt of Congress. Both claims have a common origin—
the law and custom of the British Parliament. Both per-
sisted in the United States after they came to an end in
England. Both involve the basic evil presented in bills of
attainder—punishment by a legislature as a legislature without the safeguards of a judicial trial. Every argument
against one arbitrary course of action applies to the other.

In the field of contempt, the United States Supreme
Court ruled in 1821 (in *Anderson* v. *Dunn*) that the actions of Congress could not be reviewed in the courts. The
decision was based entirely on British precedents. Eighteen
years later, in the historic British case of *Stockdale* v.
Hansard (in reality, a series of cases had that title) Lord
Chief Justice Denman and his colleagues broke with previous decisions by holding that although Parliament was
omnipotent, its omnipotence did not extend to the actions
of the individual Houses. Proceedings of the House of Commons in cases of contempt were subject to judicial review.
The Commons struck back by imprisoning the Sheriff of
Middlesex for obeying the court's order. Thus confronted,
the judges rejected a petition to set the Sheriff free on a
writ of *habeas corpus*. Mixing prudence with irony, Denman said the Court refused to act on suspicion that the
House "would suppress facts which, if discussed, might entitle the person committed to his liberty." But in a memor-

able dictum, the Chief Justice adhered to the decision in *Stockdale* v. *Hansard:*

"[That judgment] appears to me in all respects correct. The Court decided there that there was no power in this country above being questioned by law. The House of Commons then attempted to place its privilege on the footing of an unquestionable and unlimited power. . . . I endeavored to establish that the claim advanced in that case tended to a despotic power which could not be recognized to exist in this country. . . . To all of these positions I, on further consideration, adhere."

The Commons kept the Sheriff of Middlesex in jail, but Denman won the war. Never again was the validity of *Stockdale* v. *Hansard* challenged in Great Britain. Four decades passed before Denman's reasoning prevailed in the United States. Then, in *Kilbourn* v. *Thompson* (1880), the Supreme Court repudiated *Anderson* v. *Dunn* and established its power to review contempt of Congress proceedings in any case where that issue is properly presented. Justice Samuel F. Miller, speaking for the Court, gave Lord Denman full credit for the reversal:

"In the celebrated case of *Stockdale* v. *Hansard,* decided in 1839, this doctrine of the omnipotence of the House of Commons received its first serious check in a court of law. . . . Lord Denman, in a masterly opinion, concurred in by the other judges of the King's Bench, ridicules the idea of the existence of a body of laws and customs unknown and unknowable to anybody but the members of the two Houses, and holds with an incontrovertible logic that when the rights of the citizen are at stake in a court of justice, it must, if these privileges are set up to his prejudice, examine for itself into the nature and character of those laws, and decide upon their extent and effect upon the rights of the parties before the court."

This principle, Justice Miller found, had its beginnings in the High Court of Parliament, before that governing body was divided into the House of Lords and House of Commons. The High Court of bishops, lords, knights, and burgesses exercised a common jurisdiction involving impeachment, bills of attainder, and judicial review. Upon the division of the high court of Parliament, judicial review passed to the Lords, impeachment to the Commons. Both Houses jointly exercised "the power of passing bills of attainder for treason and other high crimes."

By a remarkable circumstance, Chief Justice Denman's conclusion was aided by an attempted contrast between the British and American constitutional systems. Arguing for the Commons in *Stockdale* v. *Hansard,* the British attorney general said:

"There might indeed be a Court superior to the Legislature, like the supreme court of the United States of America, which is authorized to decide on the legality of acts of Congress. . . . But here no such Court exists."

Lord Denman held in effect that such a court did exist in England, and that its power had a similar origin—in constitutional necessity to preserve free government. The United States Constitution confers no express power to annul acts of Congress which violate the provisions of that charter. The power arises from the supremacy of the Constitution and the mandate that "The judicial power shall extend to all cases in law and equity arising under this Constitution," plus the self-evident fact that law and equity cannot be maintained if Congress is free to disregard the provisions of the Constitution. Since Great Britain has no written constitution, the principle is less specific there, but the basis of it is found in the British shift from despotism to self-government.

It thus appears that from the fourteenth century down to

the present day, there has been an interlocking of impeachment and attainder in British and (more recently) American legal history. England has moved steadily toward abolition of both systems of punishment; the United States combined a constitutional prohibition of attainder with strict containment of impeachment to avoid the excesses of attainder. This wise move by the framers has been frustrated by unreasoned attempts in Congress to fasten upon the country the despotic practices of medieval England, long since abandoned by the English.

The trial of Andrew Johnson a century ago gave full warning of what lay ahead if the drift toward attainder disguised as impeachment was not halted. The uneven moves against attainder in other forms (loyalty oaths, contempt of Congress, excesses of congressional committees) mark this supposedly obsolete relic of absolutism as one of the greatest present-day threats to American liberty and to stable, orderly, free government. The remedy—a judicial check on' impeachment when it amounts to a bill of attainder—is implicit in the unanswered and unanswerable arguments of Johnson's lawyers, who saved the country from the disaster of a partisan, prejudiced impeachment. It is implicit in Hamilton's Seventy-Eighth Federalist paper, in Madison's speech on the Democratic Societies, in Marshall's opinion in *Marbury* v. *Madison*.

An attempted denial of that judicial power by act of Congress would create the precise condition described by Chief Justice Marshall as the alternative to judicial review. Said he in *Marbury* v. *Madison:*

"It is a proposition too plain to be contested, that the constitution controls any legislative act repugnant to it, OR that the legislature may alter the constitution by an ordinary law.

"Between these alternatives, there is no middle ground.

The constitution is either a superior paramount law, unchangeable by ordinary means, or it is on a level with ordinary legislative acts, and, like other acts, is alterable when the legislature shall please to alter it. If the former part of the alternative be true, then a legislative act, contrary to the constitution, is not law; if the latter part be true, then written constitutions are absurd attempts, on the part of the people, to limit a power, in its own nature, illimitable."

If the question of attainder by impeachment ever comes before the Supreme Court—as it is almost certain to do at some time—it is to be hoped that the person impeached will not be one of the members of the Court. But although this would be an embarrassment, there are overriding reasons why it would not affect the Court's decision. Should a justice be impeached for genuine high crimes or misdemeanors, his colleagues, either from public policy or to protect themselves, would be more anxious than any others to be rid of him. It is impossible to conceive of eight honest men protecting a crook or a traitor, nor will there ever be a Court containing a criminal majority protecting each other.

What would be the real effect of recognizing that such a power of review exists? It would put away forever the need to exercise that power. Congressional zealots would never venture into such plainly identifiable attainders as the Andrew Johnson impeachment or the equally partisan moves against Justice Chase and Justice Douglas—not if they knew that the constitutionality of the proceedings would be subject to impartial review in the highest judicial tribunal.

In fact, the whole medieval impeachment system could well fall into disuse, with nothing but benefit resulting. A method would have to be found, however, for dealing with that rare exception—the lower-court judge whose conduct furnishes constitutional ground for removal. Impeachment of judges disappeared from England when a merit system of selection succeeded royal favoritism. Back of that in England lies power of removal through writs of *scire facias* —judicial self-policing. Such a system has been proposed for the United States.* But what is imperatively needed is a means of preventing treatment of federal district judgeships as political patronage for members of Congress or as refuges for congressional lame ducks. This is the worst blight in our entire structure of government. Best of all would be a constitutional amendment empowering the Supreme Court or some special tribunal to remove inferior-court judges for incompetence, disability, or offenses now impeachable. It would end the ludicrous folly of tying up the Senate in these time-consuming operations of minor importance and infinite detail.

In addition, the scope of such an amendment should be broad enough to cover special cases applying to higher officials. For recognition that the "attainder clause" effectively limits impeachment to grounds permitted by the Constitution would leave one small gap in the governmental security system. House and Senate would be without power to remove a President, Vice President, or Supreme Court

---

* See Raoul Berger, "Impeachment of Judges and 'Good Behavior' Tenure," *Yale Law Journal*, July 1970. Berger's proposed system of removing inferior-court judges through writs of *scire facias* is admirable. However, one cannot accept his conclusion that power to establish such a system already exists as an "incident" to tenure "during good behavior." That would extend the reach of the power to members of the Supreme Court (which he opposes), thus turning the judicial system upside down. It would make a President constitutionally removable by a district court order if he held office for life or during good behavior. The whole edifice of removal for lapse of "good behavior," it is wise to remember, stems from a sixteenth-century British statute for removal of "ignorant and unlearned" clerks from justiceships of the peace.

justice who might suffer so complete a mental or physical breakdown that he would be unable to resign. The thought of such an occurrence, never experienced but always possible, has helped to produce the vastly greater danger inherent in unlimited, unlawful grounds of impeachment. Both the disaster of a high official's breakdown without means to remove him, and the menace of ungranted jurisdiction put forward to forestall its possibility, could be remedied by a simple, noncontroversial change in the Constitution.

Let the suggested provision for removal of inferior judges by *scire facias* be part of a larger amendment with the principal provision:

> *When the President, Vice President, or any Justice of the Supreme Court shall become physically or mentally incompetent to perform his duties, and is found by the Supreme Court to be thus physically or mentally incompetent, he may be removed from office by the process prescribed for impeachment.*

Such a provision would furnish an effective remedy entirely without stigma. The requirement of united action by House, Senate, and Supreme Court would establish a safeguard against political abuse. It would cancel the only cogent argument for arbitrary assertion of a broader power of impeachment than the Constitution sanctions. By implication, it would strengthen the restrictive force of the requirement that impeachment be only for "treason, bribery, or other high crimes and misdemeanors." It would add strength to the prohibitions of bills of attainder and *ex post facto* laws, both of which are being devitalized by the extension of impeachment into these forbidden fields.

Since political foresight hardly ever supplies a sufficient

prod to action, there is no reason to suppose that any such amendment will be submitted to the states in advance of the incentive arising from a calamity. However, House and Senate could diminish the pressures that result in unconstitutional procedures by adopting a concurrent resolution urgently called for by the tragic history of impeachment from 1797 down to the present day. Let Congress resolve that: "No President, Vice President, or civil officer of the United States shall ever be impeached for conduct which would not cause a Senator or Representative to be expelled from his seat."

Documentary Sources

William Blount (impeached 1797): *Annals of Congress,* Vol. 7, index, columns v, vi, xli, xlii; trial, Vol. 8, columns 2244–416.

John Pickering (impeached 1803): *Annals of Congress,* Vol. 12, index, columns v, xv; Vol. 8, index, viii; trial, 315–67.

Samuel Chase (impeached 1804): *Annals of Congress,* Vol. 14, index, columns iii, viii, xxi; trial, columns 92–676.

James H. Peck (impeached 1826): *Register of Debates,* Vol. VI, Part II, index, pages ii, vii; Vol. VII, index, vii; trial, Vol. VIII, index, 3–4, 9–45.

West H. Humphreys (impeached 1862): *Congressional Globe,* Vol. 32, index, pages xviii, xlviii; trial, Vol. 32, Part 4, 2942–55.

Andrew Johnson (impeached 1868): *Congressional Globe,* 40th Congress, Second Session, Part 2, index, pages cxl–cxli; Supplement, The Proceedings of the Senate sitting for the trial of Andrew Johnson, 40th Congress, Second Session.

William W. Belknap (impeached 1876): *Congressional Record,* 44th Congress, First Session, index to Parts 1–6, pages 22, 202; Part 7, Trial of W. W. Belknap.

Charles Swayne (impeached 1903): *Congressional Record,* 58th Congress, Third Session, index, page 300.

Robert W. Archbald (impeached 1912): *Congressional Record,* 62nd Congress, Second Session, index, page 23; Third Session, index, pages 12–13; record of trial, page 1051.

George W. English (impeached 1926): *Congressional Record,* 68th Congress, Second Session, Vol. 66, Part 6, index, page 65; 69th Congress, First Session, Vol. 67, Part 12, index, page 158; Vol. 68, Part 6, index, pages 9, 77.

Harold Louderback (impeached 1932): *Congressional Record,* 72nd Congress, First Session, index, page 380; 73rd Congress, First Session, index, pages 163–4.

Halsted L. Ritter (impeached 1936): *Congressional Record,* 74th Congress, Second Session, index, 324–5; trial, pages 4971–5004. Document No. 200, 74th Congress, Second Session.

Hinds–Cannon Precedents of the House of Representatives: on Blount, III, 2294; Pickering, III, 2319; Chase, III, 2342; Peck, III, 2364; Humphreys, III, 2385; Johnson, III, 2408; Belknap, III, 2444; Swayne, III, 2469; Archbald, VI, 498; English, VI, 544–5; Louderback, VI, 513.

Investigation of charges against Associate Justice William O. Douglas (1970): *Congressional Record,* April 15, April 21, 1970. Committee prints, 91st Congress, Second Session: first report by the special subcommittee on H. Res. 920 of the House Committee on the Judiciary, June 20, 1970; Legal Materials on impeachment, August 11, 1970; final report by the special subcommittee, September 17, 1970.

Index

A NOTE ABOUT THE AUTHOR

IRVING BRANT is a noted authority on constitutional history. Born in Walker, Iowa, in 1885, he was graduated from the University of Iowa in 1909. For many years he was one of the country's most influential editorial writers, for newspapers such as the St. Louis *Star-Times* and the Chicago *Sun*. His six-volume biography of James Madison, published between 1941 and 1961, is regarded as a classic. Mr. Brant has written eight other books, including a historical novel, and has contributed to magazines such as *The New Republic* and *The Nation*. He now lives with his wife in Eugene, Oregon.